VA

THE JUNIOR GREAT BOOKS PROGRAM offe[rs] high school students the opportunity to read [and discuss] the books that have come to be recognized as an essential part of a liberal education. The Great Books have been singled out in this way because they deal with fundamental situations and questions that have implications for all of us in our daily lives. They are books which repay careful and repeated reading because new meanings are constantly discovered in them.

In a Junior Great Books group, members have the opportunity to express their opinions and to hear what others have to say about the selections. The meetings are led by two adult volunteers, who have taken a Great Books Leader Training Course. They encourage the participants to agree or disagree with the authors and with each other, provided they back up their opinions with reasons based on their reading. By exchanging and testing their ideas, participants may expect to leave the meetings with an increased understanding and appreciation of the works they have discussed.

Students should find the Junior Great Books discussion program a pleasurable and stimulating activity in which they sharpen their skills in reading, thinking, speaking, and listening. We hope the program will provide a useful addition to the student's formal education and will contribute to the formation of a lifetime habit of reading and discussing the books which have enriched and helped to shape our civilization.

The Junior Great Books Program is sponsored by The Great Books Foundation, a non-profit educational organization. Since its inception in 1947, the Foundation has conducted a similar reading and discussion program for adults. The Foundation's services include training discussion leaders, organizing groups, supplying publicity materials, choosing selections, and publishing books in inexpensive boxed editions. With over 50,000 participants in more than 3,300 groups, Great Books is the largest educational program of its kind in the United States. For further information about the Foundation and its activities, write The Great Books Foundation, 5 South Wabash Avenue, Chicago 3, Illinois.

Note to Reader:

In order to increase both the enjoyment and value of your participation in The Junior Great Books Program, please remember that you are reading this book in preparation for discussion. Therefore, you should read the entire book, or at least portions of it, more than once. You may want to mark passages and make comments in the margins or on the blank pages provided in the back of the books. Some of the things you may wish to underline or write down are:

1. Ideas in the book you consider important.

2. Words or passages that you do not understand.

3. Passages with which you agree or disagree.

4. Passages about which you would like to hear the opinions of others.

5. Passages on which you would like to comment in the light of your own experience.

6. Passages which remind you of other Great Books your group has read and discussed.

This book belongs to _Grade 9_.

CAJON VALLEY UNION SCHOOL DISTRICT
LIBRARY SERVICE
EL CAJON, CALIFORNIA

JUNIOR GREAT BOOKS

SET FIVE
VOLUME ONE

HOMER, the principal figure of ancient Greek literature, is believed to have lived in Asia Minor sometime before 700 B.C. Scholars disagree about the exact period in which he lived; some place it as far back as 1150 B.C. At least seven different cities are recorded as claiming to be his birthplace. Tradition holds that he was blind. Little is known authoritatively about his life, although there are several "Lives of Homer," including some that go back to antiquity. Scholars believe that his two great epics, *The Iliad* and *The Odyssey*, were probably based on older legends and that he wrote for an aristocratic society. They have also concluded that *The Iliad* was probably written first. Homer's books came to be revered in many parts of Greece; in Athens they were an important part of a citizen's education. It is said that the law required the works of Homer "and no other poet" to be recited at the Panathenaea, a festival in honor of Athena. Aeschylus is reported to have described his own plays as "slices from the great banquets of Homer." *The Iliad* and *The Odyssey* are among the most widely read literary works of today, as they have been for three thousand years.

HOMER

The Odyssey
SELECTION

NUMBER 1
SET FIVE

THE GREAT BOOKS FOUNDATION *Chicago*

From THE ODYSSEY *by Homer.*
Translated by W. H. D. Rouse.
*Published by arrangement with Thomas Nelson and Sons Ltd. and
with The New American Library of World Literature, publishers of
Signet and Mentor Paperback Books.*

*The special contents of this edition are copyright 1963
by* THE GREAT BOOKS FOUNDATION. *This selection has been specially
edited for the Junior Great Books discussion program.*

Printed in the United States of America.

published and distributed by

THE GREAT BOOKS FOUNDATION
a non-profit corporation
5 South Wabash Avenue, Chicago 3, Illinois

THE ODYSSEY

BOOK IX

HOW ODYSSEUS VISITED THE LOTUS-EATERS AND THE CYCLOPS

THEN ODYSSEUS began his tale:

"What a pleasure it is, my lord," he said, "to hear a singer like this, with a divine voice! I declare it is just the perfection of gracious life: good cheer and good temper everywhere, rows of guests enjoying themselves heartily and listening to the music, plenty to eat on the table, wine ready in the great bowl, and the butler ready to fill your cup whenever you want it. I think that is the best thing men can have.—But you have a mind to hear my sad story, and make me more unhappy than I was before. What shall I begin with, what shall I end with? The lords of heaven have given me sorrow in abundance.

"First of all I will tell you my name, and then you may count me one of your friends if I live to reach my home, although that is far away. I am Odysseus Laërtiadês, a name well known in the world as one who is ready for any event. My home is Ithaca, that bright conspicuous isle, with Mount Neriton rising clear out of the quivering forests. Round it lie many islands clustering close, Dulichion and Samê and woody Zacynthos. My island lies low, last of all in the sea to westward, the others away towards the dawn and the rising sun. It is rough, but a nurse of good lads; I tell you there is no sweeter sight any man can see than his own country. Listen now: a radiant goddess Calypso tried to keep me by her in

1

16086

her cave, and wanted me for a husband; Circê also would have had me stay in her mansion, and a clever creature she was, and she also wanted me for a husband, but she never could win my heart. How true it is that nothing is sweeter than home and kindred, although you may have a rich house in a foreign land far away from your kindred! Ah well, but you are waiting to hear of my journey home, and all the sorrows which Zeus laid upon me after I left Troy.

"From Ilion the wind carried me to Ismaros of the Ciconians. There I destroyed the city and killed the men. We spared the women and plenty of cattle and goods, which we divided to give each man a fair share. I told the men we must show a light heel and be off, but the poor fools would not listen. Plenty of wine was drunk, plenty of sheep were killed on that beach, and herds of cattle! Meanwhile some of the enemy got away and shouted to other Ciconians, neighbours of their inland, more men and better men, who knew how to fight from the chariot against a foe, and on foot if need be.

"A multitude of these men swarmed down early in the morning, as many as leaves and flowers in the season of the year. Surely Zeus sent us a hard fate that day, to bring trouble on a lot of poor devils! They drew up near the ships, and then came volleys on both sides. All through the morning while the day grew stronger we stood our ground and held them off, although they outnumbered us; but when the sun began to change course, about ox-loosing time, the Ciconians got the upper hand and bent our line. Six men-at-arms from each vessel were killed; and the rest of us were saved alive.

"From that place we sailed onward much discouraged, but glad to have escaped death, although we had lost good companions. Yet we did not let the galleys go off, until we had called thrice on the name of each of our hapless comrades who died in that place. But Zeus Cloudgatherer sent a norwester upon our fleet with a furious tempest, bringing clouds over land and sea; and night rushed down from the sky. The ships were blown plunging along, the sails were split into shreds and tatters by the violence of the wind. We let down the sails in fear of death, and rowed the bare hulls to shore. There we lay two days and two nights on end, eating out our hearts with hardship and anxiety. But when the third day showed welcome streaks of light, we stept the masts and hoisted new sails, and sat still, while the wind drove us on and the steersman held the way. Then I might have come safe to my native land, but the sea and the current and the north-west wind caught me as I was doubling Cape Malea, and drifted me outside Cythera.

"Nine days after that I was beaten about on the sea by foul winds, and on the tenth day we made land in the country of the lotus-eaters, who get their food from flowers. We went ashore and took in water, and the men made their meal on the spot close to the ships. When we had eaten and drunk, I sent some of them to find out who the natives were: two picked men with a speaker. Before long they came across some of the lotus-eaters. However, they did no harm to the men, only gave them some of their lotus to eat. As soon as they tasted that honey-sweet fruit, they thought no more of coming back to us with news, but chose rather to stay there with the lotus-eating natives, and chew their lotus, and good-bye to home. I brought them back to the ships by main force, grumbling and complaining, and when I had them there, tied them up and stowed them under the benches. Then I ordered the rest to hurry up and get aboard, for I did not want them to have a taste of lotus and say good-bye to home. They were soon on board and sitting on their benches, and rowing away over the sea.

"From that place we sailed on in low spirits. We came next to the Cyclopians, the Goggle-eyes, a violent and lawless tribe. They trust to providence, and neither plant nor plow, but everything grows without sowing or plowing; wheat and barley and vines, which bear grapes in huge bunches, and the rain from heaven makes them grow of themselves. These Cyclopians have no parliament for debates and no laws, but they live on high mountains in hollow caves; each one lays down the law for wife and children, and no one cares for his neighbours.

"Now a low flat island lies across their harbour, not very near the land and not very far, covered with trees. In this are an infinite number of wild goats, for no man walks there to scare them away, and no hunters frequent the place to follow their toilsome trade in the forests and the hills. So it has neither flocks nor tillage; but unsown and unplowed, untrodden of men, it feeds the bleating goats. For the Goggle-eyes have no ships with their crimson cheeks, and no shipwrights among them, to build boats for them to row in and visit the cities of the world, like men who traverse the seas on their lawful occasions. Such craftsmen might have civilized the island: for it is not a bad island. It could produce all the kindly fruits of the earth; there are meadows along the shore, soft land with plenty of water; there might be no end of grapes. There is smooth land for the plow; the soil is very rich, and they might always stack a good harvest in the season of the year. There is a harbour with easy riding; no cable is wanted, no anchor-stones or stern-hawsers. You just beach your ship, and stay till the sailors have a fancy to go and the wind blows fair. Moreover, at the head of the harbour there is glorious water, a spring running out of a cave, with poplars growing all round.

"Some providence guided us in through the dark night,

with not a thing to be seen; for a thick mist was about our ships, and the moon showed no light through the clouds. At that time we did not catch a glimpse of the island: indeed we saw no long breakers rolling towards the land, before our ships ran up on the beach. When they were safe there, we lowered the sails and got out on the shore, and slept heavily until the dawn.

"As soon as dawn gleamed through the mist, we roamed about and admired the island. Then those kindly daughters of Zeus, the Nymphs, sent down goats from the hills to give us all a good meal. We lost no time, got our bows and long spears out of the ships, divided into three bands, and let fly at the quarry. Very soon God gave us as much as we wanted. I had twelve ships with me, and nine goats were given to each by lot, but ten were picked out for me alone. So all day long we sat there feasting, with plenty of meat and delicious wine. For the good red wine was not all used up yet, but some was left; when we took the Ciconian city, each crew had supplied themselves with plenty in large two-handled jars. We gazed at the country of the Goggle-eyes, which was quite close; we could see the smoke and hear the bleating of sheep and goats. When the sun set and darkness came, we lay down on the beach to sleep.

"But with the first rosy streaks of the dawn, I called a meeting and made a speech to the men. 'My good fellows,' I said, 'the rest of you stay here, while I take my ship and crew and see who these people are; whether they are wild savages who know no law, or hospitable men who know right from wrong.'

"So I went aboard and told my crew to cast loose; they were soon in their places and rowing along. The land was not far off, and when we reached it we saw a cave there on a headland close by the sea, high and shaded with laurels, in which numbers of animals were housed by night, both sheep and goats. Outside was an enclosure with high walls round it, made of great stones dug into the earth and the trunks of tall pines and spreading oaks. These were the night-quarters of a monstrous man, who was then tending his flocks a long way off by himself; he would not mix with the others, but kept apart in his own lawless company. Indeed he was a wonderful monster, not like a mortal man who eats bread, but rather like a mountain peak with trees on the top standing up alone in the highlands.

"Then I told the rest of my men to wait for me and look after the ship, but I picked out twelve of the best men I had, and we set out. I took with me a goatskin of ruby wine, delicious wine, which I had from Maron Euanthidês, priest of Apollo who was the protecting god of Ismaros. We had saved him and his wife and child out of reverence, because he lived in the sacred grove of Phoibos Apollo. I had glorious gifts from him: he gave me seven talents' weight of worked gold, he gave me a mixing-bowl of solid silver, but besides that, he gave me great jars of wine, a whole dozen of them, delicious wine, not a drop of water in it, a divine drink! Not a soul knew about this wine, none of the servants or women, except himself and his own wife and one cellarer. When they drank of this wine, he used to pour one cup of it into twenty measures of water, and a sweet scent was diffused abroad from the mixer, something heavenly; no one wanted to be an abstainer then! I had filled a skin with this wine, and brought it with me, also a bag of provisions; for from the first I had a foreboding that I should meet a man of mighty strength, but savage, knowing neither justice nor law.

"We walked briskly to the cave, but found him not at home; he was tending his fat flocks on the pasture. So we entered the cave and took a good look all round. There were baskets loaded with cheeses, there were pens stuffed full of lambs and kids. Each lot was kept in a separate place; firstlings in one, middlings in another, yeanlings in another. Every pot and pan was swimming with whey, all the pails and basins into which he did the milking. The men begged me first to let them help themselves to the cheeses and be off; next they wanted to make haste and drive the kids and lambs out of the pens and get under sail. But I would not listen—indeed it would have been much better if I had! but I wanted to see himself and claim the stranger's gift. As it turned out, he was destined to be anything but a vision of joy to my comrades.

"So we lit a fire and made our thank-offering, and helped ourselves to as many cheeses as we wanted to eat; then we sat inside till he should come back with his flocks. At last in he came, carrying a tremendous load of dry wood to give light for supper. This he threw down inside the cave with a crash that terrified us, and sent us scurrying into the corners. Then he drove his fat flocks into the cave, that is to say, all he milked, leaving the rams and billy-goats outside the cave but within the high walls of the enclosure. Then he picked up a huge great stone and placed it in the doorway: not two and twenty good carts with four wheels apiece could have lifted it off the ground, such was the size of the precipitous rock which he planted in front of the entrance. Then he sat down and milked the goats and ewes, bleating loudly, all in order, and put her young under each. Next he curdled half of the white milk and packed it into wicker baskets, leaving the other half to stand in bowls, that he might have some to drink for supper or whenever he wanted. At last after all this busy work, he lighted the fire and saw us.

" 'Who are you?' he called out. 'Where do you come from over the watery ways? Are you traders, or a lot of pirates ready to kill and be killed, bringing trouble to foreigners?'

"While he spoke, our hearts were wholly broken within us to see the horrible monster, and to hear that beastly voice. But I managed to answer him:

" 'We are Achaians from Troy, driven out of our course over the broad sea by all the winds of heaven. We meant to sail straight home, but we have lost our way altogether: such was the will of Zeus, I suppose. We have the honour to be the people of King Agamemnon Atreidês, whose fame is greatest of all men under the sky, for the strong city he sacked and the many nations he conquered. But we have found you, and come to your knees, to pray if you will give us the stranger's due or anything you may think proper to give to a stranger. Respect the gods, most noble sir; see, we are your suppliants! Strangers and suppliants have their guardian strong, God walks with them to see they get no wrong.'

"He answered me with cruel words: 'You are a fool, stranger, or you come from a long way off, if you expect me to fear gods. Zeus Almighty be damned and his blessed gods with him. We Cyclopians care nothing for them, we are stronger than they are. I should not worry about Zeus if I wanted to lay hands on you or your companions. But tell me, where did you moor your ship—far off or close by? I should be glad to know that.'

"He was just trying it on, but I knew something of the world, and saw through it; so I answered back, 'My ship was wrecked by Poseidon Earthshaker, who cast us on the rocks near the boundary of your country; the wind drove us on a lee shore. But I was saved with these others.'

"The cruel monster made no answer, but just jumped up and reached out towards my men, grabbed two like a pair of puppies and dashed them on the ground: their brains ran out and soaked into the earth. Then he cut them up limb by limb, and made them ready for supper. He devoured them like a mountain lion, bowels and flesh and marrow-bones, and left nothing. We groaned aloud, lifting our hands to Zeus, when we saw this brutal business; but there was nothing to be done.

"When Goggle-eye had filled his great belly with his meal of human flesh, washed down with a draught of milk neat, he lay and stretched himself among the sheep. But I did not lose heart. I considered whether to go near and draw my sharp sword and drive it into his breast; I could feel about till I found the place where the midriff encloses the liver. But second thoughts kept me back. We should have perished ourselves in that place, dead and done for; we could never have moved the great stone which he had planted in the doorway. So we lay groaning and awaited the dawn.

"Dawn came. He lit the fire, milked his flocks, all in order, put the young under each, then he grabbed two more men and prepared his breakfast. That done, he drove out the fat flocks, moving away the great stone with ease; but he put it back again, just as you fit cover to quiver. With many a whistle Goggle-eye turned his fat flocks to the hills; but I was left brooding and full of dark plans, longing to have my revenge if Athena would grant my prayer.

"Among all my schemes and machinations, the best plan I could think of was this. A long spar was lying beside the pen, a sapling of green olive-wood; Goggle-eye had cut it down to dry it and use as a staff. It looked to us about as large as the mast of a twenty-oar ship, some broad hoy that sails the deep sea; it was about that length and thickness. I cut off a fathom of this, and handed it over to my men to dress down. They made it smooth, then I sharpened the end and charred it in the hot fire, and hid it carefully under the dung which lay in a great mass all over the floor. Then I told the others to cast lots who should help me with the pole and rub it into his eye while he was sound asleep. The lot fell on those four whom I would have chosen myself, which made five counting me.

"In the evening, back he came with his flocks. This time he drove them all into the cave, and left none outside in the yard; whether he suspected something, or God made him do it, I do not know. Then he lifted the great stone and set it in place, sat down and milked his ewes and nannies bleating loudly, all in order, put her young under each, and when all this was done, grabbed two more men and made his meal.

"At this moment I came near to Goggle-eye, holding in my hand an ivy-wood cup full of the red wine, and I said:

" 'Cyclops, here, have a drink after that jolly meal of mans-mutton! I should like to show you what drink we had on board our ship. I brought it as a drink-offering for you, in the hope that you might have pity and help me on my way home. But you are mad beyond all bearing! Hard heart, how can you expect any other men to pay you a visit? For you have done what is not right.'

"He took it and swallowed it down. The good stuff delighted him terribly, and he asked for another drink:

" 'Oh, please give me more, and tell me your name this very minute! I will give you a stranger's gift which will make you happy! Mother earth does give us wine in huge bunches, even in this part of the world, and the rain from heaven makes them grow; but this is a rivulet of nectar and ambrosia!'

"Then I gave him a second draught. Three drinks I gave him; three times the fool drank. At last, when the wine had got into his head, I said to him in the gentlest of tones:

" 'Cyclops, do you ask me my name? Well, I will tell you, and you shall give me the stranger's due, as you promised. Noman is my name; Noman is what mother and father call me and all my friends.'

"Then the cruel monster said, 'Noman shall be last eaten of

his company, and all the others shall be eaten before him! that shall be your stranger's gift.'

"As he said this, down he slipt and rolled on his back. His thick neck drooped sideways, and all-conquering sleep laid hold on him; wine dribbled out of his gullet with lumps of human flesh, as he belched in his drunken slumbers. Then I drove the pole deep under the ashes to grow hot, and spoke to hearten my men that no one might fail me through fear.

"As soon as the wood was on the point of catching fire, and glowed white-hot, green as it was, I drew it quickly out of the fire while my men stood round me: God breathed great courage into us then. The men took hold of the stake, and thrust the sharp point into his eye; and I leaned hard on it from above and turned it round and round. As a man bores a ship's timber with an auger, while others at the lower part keep turning it with a strap which they hold at each end, and round and round it runs: so we held the fire-sharpened pole and turned it, and the blood bubbled about its hot point. The fumes singed eyelids and eyelashes all about as the eyeball burnt and the roots crackled in the fire. As a smith plunges an axe or an adze in cold water, for that makes the strength of steel, and it hisses loud when he tempers it, so his eye sizzled about the pole of olive-wood.

"He gave a horrible bellow till the rocks rang again, and we shrank away in fear. Then he dragged out the post from his eye dabbled and dripping with blood, and threw it from him, wringing his hands in wild agony, and roared aloud to the Cyclopians who lived in caves round about among the windy hills. They heard his cries, and came thronging from all directions, and stood about the cave, asking what his trouble was:

" 'What on earth is the matter with you, Polyphemos?' they called out. 'Why do you shout like this through the night and wake us all up? Is any man driving away your flocks against your will? Is any one trying to kill you by craft or main force?'

"Out of the cave came the voice of mighty Polyphemos: 'O my friends, Noman is killing me by craft and not by main force!'

"They answered him in plain words:

" 'Well, if no man is using force, and you are alone, there's no help for a bit of sickness when heaven sends it; so you had better say your prayers to Lord Poseidon your father!'

"With these words away they went, and my heart laughed within me, to think how a mere nobody had taken them all in with my machinomanations!

"But the Cyclops, groaning and writhing in agony, fumbled about with his hands until he found the stone and pushed it away from the entrance. There he sat with his hands outspread to catch any one who tried to go out with the animals. A great fool he must have thought me! But I had been casting about what to do for the best, if I could possibly find some escape from death for my comrades and myself. All kinds of schemes and machinations I wove in my wits, for it was life or death, and perdition was close by. The plan that seemed to me best was this. The rams were well grown, large and fine, with coats of rich dark wool. In dead silence I tied them together with twisted withies, which the monster used for his bed. I tied them in threes, with a man under the middle one, while the two others protected him on each side. So three carried each of our fellows; but for myself—there was one great ram, the finest of the whole flock; I threw my arms over his back, and curled myself under his shaggy belly, and there I lay turned upwards, with only my hands to hold fast by the wonderful fleece in patience. So we all waited anxiously for the dawn.

"At last the dawn came. The rams and billies surged out to pasture, but the nannies and ewes unmilked went bleating round the pens; for their udders were full to bursting. Their master still tormented with pain felt over the backs of all the animals as they passed out; but the poor fool did not notice how my men were tied under their bellies. Last of all the great ram stalked to the door, cumbered with the weight of his wool and of me and my teeming mind. Polyphemos said as he pawed him over:

" 'Hullo, why are you last to-day, you lazy creature? It is not your way to let them leave you behind! No, no, you go first by a long way to crop the fresh grass, stepping high and large, first to drink at the river, first all eagerness to come home in the evening; but now last! Are you sorry perhaps for your master's eye, which a damned villain has blinded with his cursed companions, after he had fuddled me with wine? Noman! who hasn't yet escaped the death in store for him, I tell him that! If you only had sense like me, if you could only speak, and tell me where the man is skulking from my vengeance! Wouldn't I beat his head on the ground, wouldn't his brains go splashing all over the place! And then I should have some little consolation for the trouble which this nobody of a Noman has brought upon me!'

"So he let the ram go from him out of the cave. A little way from the cave and its enclosure, I shook myself loose first from under my ram; then I freed my companions, and with all speed we drove the fat animals trotting along, often looking round, until we reached our ship. Glad indeed our friends were to see us, all of us that were left alive; they lamented the others, and made such a noise that I had to stop it, frowning at them and shaking my head. I told them to look sharp and throw on board a number of the fleecy beasts, and get away. Soon they were in their places paddling along; but when we were about as far off from the shore as a man can shout, I called out in mockery:

"'I say, Cyclops! He didn't turn out to be such a milksop after all, did he, when you murdered his friends, and gobbled them up in your cave? Your sins were sure to find you out, you cruel brute! You had no scruple to devour your guests in your own house, therefore vengeance has fallen upon you from Zeus and the gods in heaven!'

"This made him more furious than ever. He broke off the peak of a tall rock and threw it; the rock fell in front of the ship; the sea splashed and surged up as it fell; it raised a wave which carried us back to the land, and the rolling swell drove the ship right upon the shore. I picked up a long quant and pushed her off, and nodded to the men as a hint to row hard and save their lives. You may be sure they put their backs into it! When we were twice as far as before, I wanted to shout again to Goggle-eye, although my comrades all round tried to coax me not to do it—

"'Foolhardy man! Why do you want to provoke the madman? Just now he threw something to seaward of us and drove back the ship to land, and we thought all was up with us. And if he had heard one of us speaking or making a sound, he would have thrown a jagged rock and smashed our timbers and our bones to smithereens! He throws far enough!'

"But I was determined not to listen, and shouted again in my fury:

"'I say, Cyclops! if ever any one asks you who put out your ugly eye, tell him your blinder was Odysseus, the conqueror of Troy, the son of Laërtês, whose address is in Ithaca!'

"When he heard this he gave a loud cry, and said, 'Upon my word, this is the old prophecy come true! There was a soothsayer here once, a fine tall fellow, Telemos Eurymedês, a famous soothsayer who lived to old age prophesying amongst our people. He told me what was to happen, that I should lose my sight at the hands of Odysseus. But I always expected that some tall handsome fellow would come this way, clothed in mighty power. Now a nobody, a weakling, a whippersnapper, has blinded my eye after fuddling me with wine! Come to me, dear Odysseus, and let me give you the stranger's gift, let me beseech the worshipful Earthshaker to grant you a happy voyage! For I have the honour to be his son, and he declares he is my father. He will cure me, if he chooses, all by himself, without the help of blessed gods or mortal man.'

"I answered at once, 'I wish I could kill you and send you to hell as surely as no one will ever unblind your eye, not even the Earthshaker!'

"At this he held out his hand to heaven, and prayed to Lord Poseidon:

" 'Hear me, Poseidon Earthholder Seabluehair! If I am truly thy son, and thou art indeed my father, grant that Odysseus the conqueror of Troy—the son of Laërtês—whose address is in Ithaca, may never reach his home! But if it is his due portion to see his friends and come again to his tall house and his native land, may he come there late and in misery, in another man's ship, may he lose all his companions, and may he find tribulation at home!'

"This was his prayer, and Seabluehair heard it. Then once again he lifted a stone greater than the other, and circled it round his head, gathering all his vast strength for the blow, and flung it; down it fell behind our ship, just a little, just missed the end of the steering-oar. The sea splashed and surged up as it fell, and the wave carried her on and drove her to shore on the island.

"When we came safe to the island, where the other ships were waiting for us, we found our companions in great anxiety, hoping against hope. We drew up our ship on the sand, and put the sheep of old Goggle-eye ashore, and divided them so as to give every one a fair share. But by general consent the great ram was given to me. I sacrificed him on the beach to Zeus Cronidês; clouds and darkness are round about him, and he rules over all. I made my burnt-offering, but Zeus regarded it not; for as it turned out, he intended that all my tight ships and all my trusty companions should be destroyed.

"We spent the rest of the day until sunset in feasting, eating full and drinking deep; and when the sun set and darkness came on, we lay to rest on the seashore. Then at dawn I directed the men in all haste to embark and throw off the moorings. They were soon aboard and rowing away in good fettle over the sea.

"So we fared onwards, thankful to be alive, but sorrowing for our comrades whom we had lost.

BOOK X

THE ISLAND OF THE WINDS;
THE LAND OF THE MIDNIGHT SUN; CIRCÊ

"WE CAME NEXT to the island of Aiolia. There lived Aiolos Hippotadês, a friend of the immortal gods, in a floating island: right round it was built a brazen wall unbreakable, and the rock ran up smooth and straight. Aiolos had a family of twelve children, six daughters, and six sons in their prime: the daughters he had given to the sons as wives. All these live together, and dine with their father and their excellent mother; there is always a fine spread of vittles in infinite variety. All day and every day the house is full of the steam of cooking, and the courtyard resounds with busy noise: all night they sleep beside their faithful wives on bedsteads of neat joinery, covered with blankets and rugs.

"We entered this city with its fine houses, and there spent a whole month as guests. Aiolos wanted to know all about Ilion, and the Achaian fleet, and how they returned home; and I told him the whole history from beginning to end.

"When at last I spoke of leaving, and asked him for help on our way, he was glad to consent, and did everything he could. He gave me the skin of a nine-year ox, which he flayed for us and made into a bag; and in this he bottled up the blustering winds. For Cronion had appointed him to be manager of the winds, to hold them or to let them go as he liked. On board my ship he tied up the bag with wire of shining silver, so tight that not a breath could blow out: but he left the west wind free to blow, that it might carry our ships along. As it turned out this was of no use, for we spoilt all by our own folly.

17

"Nine days we sailed all day and all night: on the tenth day our native land came in sight. We came so close that we could see them tending their fires. All that time I had held the sheet in my hand and let no one else touch it, to make sure of a quicker passage home; but when I saw the island I fell into a deep sleep, for I was tired out.

"Then the men began to talk to one another, said there must be gold and silver in that bag, presents from the generous Aiolos Hippotadês; and this is the sort of thing they were whispering:

" 'Upon my word, the man is a prime favourite wherever he goes! Plenty of treasures from the spoils of Troy, and we who travelled the same road come home with empty hands! Now again here is Aiolos obliging him with more generous gifts. Here, quick, let's look and see what he has got, how much gold and silver there is in this bag!'

"A scandalous motion, but it was passed. They opened the bag, the winds leaped out; at once a gale caught them, and carried them off to sea tearing their hair as they left their native land behind. This waked me up; I did not know what to do, whether to throw myself overboard and be drowned, or grin and bear it in the land of the living. Well, I just bore it and stayed where I was. I covered my head and lay down, while the ships were driven by the gale back to the Isle of Aiolos, amid the lamentations of my companions.

"So we went ashore, and took in fresh water, and the men had their meal beside the ships. When we had finished, I took with me a herald and one other, and went on to the house of Aiolos. We found him feasting with his wife and children. When we entered the hall, and sat on the threshold near the door, they called out in great astonishment:

" 'What has brought you here, Odysseus? What ill luck has touched you? Surely we did everything we could to help you, that you might return safely to your native land, or anywhere else you wanted to go?'

"I answered sorrowfully, 'Everything has been spoilt by the fault of my men, and sleep on the top of that, confound it! Do help us, friends: you have the power.'

"My coaxing was of no use: they were dumbfounded, and the father said, 'Get out of this island at once, you miserable sinner! It is not permitted to comfort the enemy of the blessed gods! Get out of this! You are the gods' enemy come to my doors!'

"Thus he turned me out of his house in deep distress.

"From that place we sailed on disheartened. The spirit of the men was worn out by the labour of rowing, all their own fault! for there was no wind to help us now.

"Six days we carried on, all night and all day. On the seventh we reached the lofty stronghold of Lamos, Lais-trygonian Telepylos, where herdsman hails herdsman as one brings in his droves and the other answers as he drives out his. There a man who could do without sleep, could earn double wages, one by minding cattle, one by pasturing sheep: for the paths of day and night are close together.

"We entered a fine harbour, with precipitous cliffs running all round. At the mouth are two headlands projecting front to front, and the entry is narrow. All the others steered their ships in, and moored them inside the harbour close together (for there were no waves rising inside, large or small, only white calm all round); but I alone made fast my ship outside, at the very end of the point, hitching ropes over the rocks.

"Then I climbed the cliff and stood still to get a good view. There was no arable land or garden to be seen, but we saw smoke rising in the air. So I sent some men to find out who the natives were, two picked men with a third as their spokesman.

They went ashore, and proceeded along a levelled road which was used by carts to carry down wood from the hills into the city. They came across a girl close to the city, drawing water, the sturdy daughter of Laistrygonian Antiphatês. She had come down to a running spring named Artaciê, from which they used to get water for the city. The men stopt and asked who was king in those parts, and who the people were. She answered at once, and pointed out her father's lofty roof.

"When they entered the house, there they found his wife, a woman as big as the peak of a mountain, and they hated her at sight. She sent at once to summon her husband Antiphatês from the town-meeting. He gave them a murderous reception: one he grabbed at once and prepared for supper, the other two ran away and managed to get back to the ships. But the monster made a hue-and-cry through the city. Out came the Laistrygonians rushing from every direction in thousands, great inhuman wretches like giants. They threw showers of stones from the cliffs, each as big as a man could lift, and a mighty din there was, smashing of ships and crushing of men; the giants speared them like fishes and carried them home for a horrid supper.

"While this massacre was going on in the deep harbour, I drew my sword and cut the hawsers of my ship, and told my men to put their backs into if they wanted to save their lives; then row they did, with the fear of death to help them. We blessed the open sea when we got clear of those grim rocks; my ship was the only one which escaped, all the rest were lost.

"From that place we sailed on, glad enough to have come off with our lives, but sad to lose our companions. Next we reached the island of Aiaia. There Circê lived, a terrible goddess with lovely hair, who spoke in the language of men, own sister to murderous Aietas; their father was Helios, who gives light to mankind, and their mother was Persê, a daughter of Oceanos. We brought our ship to the shore in silence, and some providence guided us into a harbour where ships could lie. There we spent two days and two nights on shore, eating out our hearts with weariness and woe.

"On the third day, as soon as dawn showed the first streaks of light, I took spear and sword and climbed to a high place, where I had a look round to see if there was any one about or any voice to be heard. Standing on the top of a rock, I saw smoke rising into the air from the house where Circê lived in the middle of thick bushes and trees.

"When I saw the smoke glowing, I considered whether I should go and inquire. The best plan seemed to be that I should return first to our ship on the shore and give the men something to eat, and then send out to inquire. Just as I came near to the ship, some god must have pitied me there so lonely, and sent me a stag with towering antlers right on my path: he was going down to the river from his woodland range to drink, for the sun's heat was heavy on him. As he came out, I struck him on the spine in the middle of the back, and the spear ran right through: down he fell in the dust with a moan, and died. I set my foot on him and drew out the spear from the wound. Then I laid the body flat on the ground, and pulled a quantity of twigs and withies, which I plaited across and twisted into a strong rope of a fathom's length: with this rope I tied together the legs of the great creature, and strung him over my neck, and so carried him down to the ship, leaning upon my spear; I could not have carried him on the shoulder with one hand, for he was a huge beast.

"I threw him down in front of the ship, and cheered up my friends with encouraging words as I turned from one to another. 'We are not going to die yet, my friends, for all our troubles: we shall not see the house of Hadês before our day comes. While there's food and drink in the ship, don't let us forget to eat! we need not die of starvation, at all events!'

"They were all sitting about with their faces muffled up in their cloaks; but at my words they threw off the cloaks, and got up quickly to stare at the stag lying on the beach; for he was a huge beast. When they had feasted their eyes on the welcome sight, they began to think of another kind of feast; so they swilled their hands in due form, and got him ready. All day long until sunset we sat enjoying ourselves with our meat and wine; and when the sun went down and the darkness came, we lay down to sleep on the seashore.

"As soon as morning dawned, I called my companions together and addressed them:

" 'My friends, we do not know east from west, we don't know where the sun rises to give light to all mankind, and where he goes down under the earth. Well, then, what are we to do? We must try to think of something at once, and for my part, I can't think of anything. I have just been up on the cliffs to look around. We are on some island in the middle of the sea, with no land in sight. The island is flat, and I saw smoke rising in the air above a coppice of bushes and trees.'

"When I said this, their hearts were crushed with foreboding: for they remembered the doings of Laistrygonian Antiphatês, and the violence of that audacious cannibal the goggle-eye Cyclops. The tears ran down their cheeks, and much good it did to weep!

"However, I divided them into two parts of equal number, and chose a captain for each: one I took myself, the other I gave to an excellent man, Eurylochos. Quickly then we shook lots in a helmet, and out leapt the lot of Eurylochos. Off he went, with his two-and-twenty men, groaning and grumbling, and we were left groaning and grumbling behind.

"They found in a dell the house of Circê, well built with shaped stones, and set in a clearing. All round it were wolves and lions of the mountains, really men whom she had bewitched by giving them poisonous drugs. They did not attack the men, but ramped up fawning on them and wagging their long tails, just like a lot of dogs playing about their master when he comes out after dinner, because they know he has always something nice for them in his pocket. So these wolves and lions with their sharp claws played about and pawed my men, who were frightened out of their wits by the terrible creatures.

"They stopt at the outer doors of the courtyard, and heard the beautiful goddess within singing in a lovely voice, as she worked at the web on her loom, a large web of incorruptible stuff, a glorious thing of delicate gossamer fabric, such as goddesses make. The silence was broken by Politês, who was nearest and dearest to me of all my companions, and the most trusty. He said:

" 'Friends, I hear a voice in the house, some woman singing prettily at the loom, and the whole place echoes with it. Goddess or woman, let's go in and speak to her.'

"Then they called her loudly. She came out at once, and opened the shining doors, and asked them to come in; they all followed her, in their innocence, only Eurylochos remained behind, for he suspected a trap. She gave them all comfortable seats, and made them a posset, cheese and meal and pale honey mixt with Pramneian wine; but she put dangerous drugs in the mess, to make them wholly forget their native land. When they had swallowed it, she gave them a tap of her wand at once and herded them into pens; for they now had pigs' heads and grunts and bristles, pigs all over except that their minds were the same as before. There they were then, miserably shut up in the pigsty. Circê threw them a lot of beechnuts and acorns and cornel-beans to eat, such as the earth-bedded swine are used to.

"But Eurylochos came back to the ship, to tell the tale of

his companions and their unkind fate. At first he could not utter a word, he was so dumbfounded with this misfortune; his eyes were full of tears, his mind foreboded trouble. At last when we were fairly flummoxed with asking questions, he found his tongue and told us how all his companions had come to grief.

" 'We went out into the wood, as you told us, most renowned chief; found a well-built house in a dell, and there some one was singing loudly as she worked the loom, goddess or woman: they called to her. She came out at once and opened the doors and asked them in: they all followed in the simplicity of their hearts, but I stayed behind because I suspected a trap. They all disappeared at once, not a soul was to be seen, and I stayed there a long time to spy.'

"When he said this, at once I slung my sword over my shoulders, the large one, bronze with silver knobs, and the bow with it, and told him to go back with me and show me the way. But he threw his arms about my knees and begged and prayed without disguise—'Don't take me there, my prince; I don't want to go. Let me stay here. I am sure you will never come back again, nor will any one who goes with you. Let us get away with those who are here while we can: we have still a chance to escape the day of destruction!'

"But I answered, 'Very well, Eurylochos, you may stay here in this place, eat and drink beside the ship. But as for me, go I must, and go I will.'

"So I made my way up from the sea-side. But just as I was on the point of entering the sacred dell and finding the house of that mistress of many spells, who should meet me but Hermês with his golden rod: he looked like a young man with the first down on his lip, in the most charming time of youth. He grasped my hand, and said:

" 'Whither away again, you poor fellow, alone on the hills,

in a country you do not know? Your companions are shut up yonder in Circê's, like so many pigs cosy in their pigsties. Are you going to set them free? Why, I warn you that you will never come back, you will stay here with the others.—All right, I will help you and keep you safe. Here, take this charm, and then you may enter the house of Circê: this will keep destruction from your head.

" 'I will reveal to you all the malign arts of Circê. She will make you a posset, and put drugs in the mess. But she will not be able to bewitch you for all that; for the good charm which I will give you will foil her. I will tell you exactly what to do.

" 'As soon as Circê gives you a tap with her long rod, draw your sword at once and rush upon her as if you meant to kill her. She will be terrified. . . .'

"With these words Argeiphontês handed me the charm which he had pulled out of the soil, and explained its nature. The root was black, but the flower was milk-white. The gods call it moly: it is hard for mortals to find it, but the gods can do all things.

"Then Hermês departed through the woody island to high Olympos; but I went on to Circê's house, and I mused deeply as I went. I stood at the doors; as I stood I called loudly, and the beautiful goddess heard. Quickly she came out and opened the doors, and I followed her much troubled.

"She led me to a fine carven chair covered with silver knobs, with a footstool for my feet. Then she mixt me a posset, and dropt in her drugs with her heart full of wicked hopes. I swallowed it, but it did not bewitch me; then she gave me a tap with her wand, and said:

" 'Now then, to the sty with you, and join your companions!'

"I drew my sharp sword and leapt at Circê as though to kill

her. She let out a loud shriek, and ran up and embraced my knees, and blurted out in dismay:

" 'Who are you, where do you come from in the wide world? Where is your city, who are your parents? I am amazed that you have swallowed my drugs and you are not bewitched. Indeed, there never was another man who could stand these drugs once he had let them pass his teeth! But you must have a mind that cannot be bewitched. Surely you are Odysseus, the man who is never at a loss! Argeiphontês Goldenrod used to say that you would come on your way from Troy in a ship. . . .'

"Then she led me to the fine carven seat, and set a footstool under my feet, and invited me to fall to. But this displeased me; I sat still half-dazed, and my heart was full of foreboding.

"When Circê noticed that I sat still and did not touch the vittles, when she saw how deeply I was troubled, she came near and spoke her mind plainly:

" 'Why do you sit there like a dumb man, Odysseus, and eat your heart out instead of eating your dinner? I suppose you expect some other treachery! You need not be afraid; I have sworn you a solemn oath.'

"I answered, 'Ah, Circê! What man with any decent feeling could have the heart to taste food and drink, until he should see his friends free and standing before his eyes? If you really mean this invitation to eat and drink, set them free, that I may see my friends before my eyes!'

"Then Circê took her wand in hand, and walked through the hall, and opened the doors of the sty, and drove them out, looking like a lot of nine-year hogs. As they stood there, she went among them and rubbed a new drug upon each; then the bristles all dropt off which the pernicious drug had grown upon their skin. They became men once more, younger than they were before, and handsomer and taller.

"They knew me, and each grasped my hand; they sobbed aloud for joy till the hall rang again with the noise, and even the goddess was touched. She came close to me, and said:

" 'Prince Laërtiadês, Odysseus never at fault! Go down to the seashore where your ship lies. First of all draw up the ship on the beach, and stow all your goods and tackle in a cave; then come back yourself and bring the rest of your companions with you.'

"So I went; and when I reached the shore, I found my companions sitting beside the ship in deep distress. But as soon as they saw me, they were like so many calves in a barnyard, skipping about a drove of cows as they come back to the midden after a good feed of grass; they cannot keep in their pens, but frolic round their dams lowing in a deafening chorus. So the men crowded round me, with tears running down over their cheeks; they felt as glad as if they had come back to their native land, to rugged Ithaca, their home where they were born and bred; and they cried out from their hearts:

" 'You are back again, my prince! How glad we are, as glad as if we had come safe home to Ithaca! Now do tell us what has become of our companions!'

"I answered gently, 'First of all we will draw up the ship on shore, and store the tackle and all our belongings in some cave. Then bestir yourselves and come with me, all of you, and you shall see your companions in the sacred house of Circê, eating and drinking. They have enough and to spare.'

"At once they set about the work. And now what should I see but Eurylochos alone trying to stop them! He made no secret of his thoughts:

" 'Oh, your poor fools!' he cried out, 'where are we going? Do you want to run your heads into trouble? Go to Circê's

house, and let her turn you all into lions or wolves to keep
watch for her whether we like it or not? Just Cyclops over
again, when our fellows went into his yard, and this same
bold Odysseus with them! It was only his rashness that
brought them to destruction!'

"When I heard this, I thought for a moment that I would
draw my sword and cut off his head, and let it roll on the
ground, for all he was my near relation. But the others held
me back and did their best to soften me:

" 'Let us leave the man here, prince, if you please, let him
stay by the ship and look after the ship. Lead the way! We
are going with you to Circê's house!'

"Then away they went up from the shore. Indeed, Eury-
lochos would not be left behind; he came too, for he had a
terror of my rough tongue.

"Then Circê gave a bath in her house to my companions,
and had them rubbed with olive oil, and gave them tunics
and woollen wraps. We found all the others feasting merrily
in the hall. When they saw one another face to face, and
knew one another, their feelings were too much for them;
they made such a noise that the roof rang again. And the
radiant goddess came up to me, and said:

" 'No more lamentations now, Odysseus! I know myself
how many hardships you have suffered on the seas, and how
many cruel enemies have attacked you on land. Now then,
eat your food and drink your wine until you become as gay
as when you first left your rugged home in Ithaca. Just now
you are withered and down-hearted, you can't forget your
dismal wanderings. Your feelings are not in tune with good
cheer, for assuredly you have suffered much.'

"We took her advice; and there we remained for a whole
year, with plenty to eat and good wine to drink.

"But when the year was past and the seasons came round
again, my companions called me aside, and said:

" 'Good heavens, have you forgotten home altogether? Do remember it, if it is really fated that you shall have a safe return to your great house and your native land!'

" . . . I entreated her earnestly, and she listened to what I had to say: 'Keep the promise you made me, Circê, that you would help me on my homeward way. My mind is set upon it, and my companions' too. They were worrying about it, and grumbling all round me when you are not by.'

"She answered: 'Prince Laërtiadês, never baffled Odysseus! I would not have you remain in my house unwillingly. But there is another journey you must make first. You must go to the house of Hadês and awful Persephoneia, to ask directions from Teiresias the blind Theban seer. His mind is still sound, for even in death Persephoneia has left him his reason; he alone has sense, and others are flitting shadows.'

"This fairly broke my heart. I groaned, and I no longer cared to live and see the light of the sun. But when I had worked off my feelings by groaning and writhing, I said to her:

" 'Oh Circê! Who will be our guide to that place? No one has ever travelled to Hadês in a ship!'

"The beautiful goddess answered, 'You need not hang about the ship and wait till a guide turns up. Set your mast, hoist your sail, and sit tight: the North Wind will take you along.

" 'When you have crossed over the ocean, you will see a low shore, and the groves of Persephoneia, tall poplars and fruit-wasting willows; there beach your ship beside deep-eddying Oceanos, and go on yourself to the mouldering house of Hadês.

" 'There into Acheron the river of pain two streams flow, Pyriphlegethon blazing with fire, and Cocytos resounding with lamentation, which is a branch of the hateful water of Styx: a rock is there, by which the two roaring streams unite.

Draw near to this, brave man, and be careful to do as I bid you. Dig a pit of about one cubit's length along and across, and pour into it a drink-offering for All Souls, first with honey and milk, then with fine wine, the third time with water: sprinkle over it white barley-meal. Pray earnestly to the empty shells of the dead; promise that if you return to Ithaca you will sacrifice to them a farrow cow, the best you have, and heap the burning pile with fine things, and to Teiresias alone in a different place you will dedicate the best black ram you have in your flocks. After that, when you have made your prayers to the goodly company of the dead, sacrifice a black ram and a black ewe, turning their heads down towards Erebos, then turn back yourself and move towards the ocean shore; the souls of the dead who have passed away will come in crowds.

" 'Then call your companions, and bid them flay and burn the bodies which lie slaughtered, and pray to the gods, to mighty Hadês and awful Persephoneia. Draw your sword and sit still, but let none of the empty shells of the dead approach the blood before you ask Teiresias what you want to know. The seer will come at once, and he will tell you the way and the measure of your path, and how you may return home over the fish-giving sea.'

"Even as she spoke, the Dawn came enthroned in gold. Circê gave me tunic and cloak to wear, and herself put on a white shining robe, delicate and lovely, with a fine girdle of gold about her waist, and drew a veil over her head. I went through the house and aroused my companions, speaking gently to each man as I stood by him:

" 'Sleep is sweet, but now, no more drowsy slumber! Let us go! Circê has told me what to do.'

"They obeyed me, full of courage. But even there we had trouble before we left. One of us, Elpenor, the youngest of all, one not so very valiant in war or steady in mind, had been sleeping by himself on the roof to get cool, being heavy with wine. He heard the noise and bustle of the men moving about, and jumped up in a hurry, but his poor wits forgot to come down again by the long ladder. He fell off the roof and broke his neck, and his soul went down to Hadês.

"When the men had all come, I said to them, 'No doubt you think we are going straight home; but Circê has marked out another road for us, to the house of Hadês and awful Persephoneia.'

"When I said this it fairly broke their hearts; they sat down where they were, and groaned and tore their hair. But it did them no good to lament.

"While we were on the way to our ship in sorrow and mourning, Circê had got there before us and left fastened near the ship a black ram and ewe. She slipt past us easily. Who could set eyes on a god if he did not wish it, going this way or coming that way?

BOOK XI

HOW ODYSSEUS VISITED THE KINGDOM OF THE DEAD

"WHEN WE reached our ship lying on the beach, the first thing we did was to launch her into the sea; then we set up mast and sail, and taking the ram and ewe we embarked in no happy mind. The radiant goddess Circê sent a sail-filling wind behind us, a good companion for a voyage. We made all shipshape aboard, and sat tight: wind and helmsman kept her on her course. All day long we ran before the wind, with never a quiver on the sail; then the sun set, and all the ways grew dark.

"We came at last to the deep stream of Oceanos which is the world's boundary. There is the city of the Cimmerian people, wrapt in mist and cloud. Blazing Helios never looks down on them with his rays, not when he mounts into the starry sky nor when he returns from sky to earth; but abominable night is for ever spread over those unhappy mortals. There we beached our ship and put the animals ashore, and we walked along the shore until we came to the place which Circê had described.

"Perimedês and Eurylochos held fast the victims, while I drew my sword and dug the pit, a cubit's length along and across. I poured out the drink-offering for All Souls, first with honey and milk, then with fine wine, and the third time with water, and I sprinkled white barley-meal over it. Earnestly I prayed to the empty shells of the dead, and promised that when I came to Ithaca, I would sacrifice to them in my own house a farrow cow, the best I had, and heap fine things on

32

the blazing pile; to Teiresias alone in a different place I would dedicate the best black ram among my flocks.

"When I had made prayer and supplication to the company of the dead, I cut the victims' throats over the pit, and the red blood poured out. Then the souls of the dead who had passed away came up in a crowd from Erebos: young men and brides, old men who had suffered much, and tender maidens to whom sorrow was a new thing; others killed in battle, warriors clad in bloodstained armour. All this crowd gathered about the pit from every side, with a dreadful great noise, which made me pale with fear.

"Then I told my men to take the victims which lay there slaughtered, to flay them and burn them, and to pray to mighty Hadês and awful Persephoneia; I myself with drawn sword sat still, and would not let the empty shells of the dead come near the blood until I had asked my questions of Teiresias.

"First came the soul of my comrade Elpenor, for he had not yet been buried in the earth. We had left his body at Circê's house, unmourned and unburied, since other tasks were pressing. I was moved with pity for him, and my tears fell as I asked him simply:

" 'Elpenor, how came you to the gloomy west? You have beaten our ship with only your feet to walk on!'

"He answered with a groan:

" 'I was done for by bad luck and a mort of drink! I slept on Circê's roof, and forgot to climb down by the long ladder, fell head over heels off the roof, broke my neck, and my soul came down to Hadês. Now I beseech you by those who are not here, those you left behind you, by your wife and your father, who cared for you as a child, by Telemachos your only son, whom you left at home—remember me, my prince, when you reach Aiaia, for I know you will touch there on your way back from Hadês. Do not leave me unmourned and unburied; do not desert me, or I may draw God's vengeance upon you! Burn me with all my arms, and pile up a barrow on the shore of the grey sea, that in days to come men may hear the story of an unhappy man; do this for me, and plant my oar on the mound, the same oar which I used when I rowed with my companions.'

"I heard, and answered, 'Be sure I will do this for you, my unhappy friend.'

"As we exchanged these sad words, I stood on one side holding my drawn sword over the blood, and my friend's phantom on the other, telling his long story.

"Then came the soul of my dead mother, Anticleia daughter of the brave Autolycos; she was alive when I left Ithaca on my voyage to sacred Ilion. My tears fell when I saw her, and I was moved with pity; but all the same, I would not let her come near the blood before I had asked my questions of Teiresias.

"Then came the soul of Theban Teiresias, holding a golden rod. He knew me, and said, 'What brings you here, unhappy man, away from the light of the sun, to visit this unpleasing place of the dead? Move back from the pit, hold off your sharp sword, that I may drink of the blood and tell you the truth.'

"As he spoke, I stept back from the pit, and pushed my sword into the scabbard. He drank of the blood, and only then spoke as the prophet without reproach:

" 'You seek to return home, mighty Odysseus, and home is sweet as honey. But God will make your voyage hard and dangerous; for I do not think the Earthshaker will fail to see you, and he is furious against you because you blinded his son. Nevertheless, you may all get safe home still, although not without suffering much, if you can control yourself and your companions when you have traversed the sea as far as the island of Thrinacia. There you will find the cattle and sheep of Helios, who sees all things and hears all things.

" 'If you sail on without hurting them you may come safe to Ithaca, although not without suffering much. But if you do them hurt, then I foretell destruction for your ship and your crew; and if you can escape it yourself, you will arrive late and miserable, all your companions lost, in the ship of a stranger. You will find trouble in your house, proud blustering men who devour your substance and plague your wife to marry and offer their bridal gifts. But you shall exact retribution from these men.

" 'When you have killed them in your hall, whether by craft or open fight with the cold steel, you must take an oar with you, and journey until you find men who do not know the sea nor mix salt with their food; they have no crimson-cheeked ships, no handy oars, which are like so many wing-feathers to a ship. I will give you an unmistakable token which you cannot miss. When a wayfarer shall meet you and tell you that is a winnowing shovel on your shoulder, fix the oar in the ground, and make sacrifice to King Poseidon, a ram, a bull, and a boar-pig; then return home and make solemn sacrifice to the immortal gods who rule the broad heavens, every one in order. Death shall come to you from the sea, death ever so peaceful shall take you off when comfortable old age shall be your only burden, and your people shall be happy round you. That which I tell you is true.'

"I answered him, 'Ah well, Teiresias, that is the thread which the gods have spun, and I have no say in the matter. But here is something I want to ask, if you will explain it to me. I see over there the soul of my dead mother. She remains in silence near the blood, and she would not look at the face of her own son or say a word to him. Tell me, prince, how may she know me for what I am?'

"He answered, 'I will give you an easy rule to remember. If you let any one of the dead come near the blood, he will tell you what is true; if you refuse, he will go away.'

"When he had said this, the soul of Prince Teiresias returned into the house of Hadês, having uttered his oracles. But I stayed where I was until my mother came near and drank the red blood. At once she knew me, and made her meaning clear with lamentable words:

" 'My love, how did you come down to the cloudy gloom, and you alive? It is hard for the living to see this place. There are great rivers between, and terrible streams, Oceanos first of all, which no one can ever cross by walking but only if he has a well-found ship. Are you on your way from Troy, have you been wandering about with ship and crew all this time? Haven't you ever been back to Ithaca, and seen your wife in your own house?'

"I answered, 'Dear mother, necessity has brought me to the house of Hadês, for I had to consult the soul of Teiresias the Theban. I have not been near Achaia nor set foot in our country. I have been driven about incessantly in toil and trouble, ever since I first sailed with King Agamemnon for Troy, to see its fine horses and to fight with its people.

" 'But do tell me, really and truly, what was the cause of your death? how did you die? Was it a long disease? or did Artemis Archeress kill you with her gentle shafts? And tell me about my father and the son I left behind me: do they still hold my honours and my possessions, or have they passed to some other man because people think I will never return? And tell me of my own wedded wife, what she thinks and what she means to do. Does she remain with the boy and keep all safe, or has she already married the best man who offered?'

"My beloved mother answered at once, 'Aye indeed, she does remain in your house. She has a patient heart; but her nights and days are consumed with tears and sorrow. Your honours and your possessions have not yet been taken away by any man, but Telemachos holds your demesne and attends the public banquets as a ruling prince ought to do, for they all invite him.

" 'But your father stays there in the country and never comes to town. His bedding is not glossy rugs and blankets on a bedstead, but in winter he sleeps among the hinds in the house, in the dust beside the fire, and wears poor clothes: when summer comes and blooming autumn, he lies on the ground anywhere about the slope of his vineyard, on a heap of fallen leaves. There he lies sorrowing and will not be comforted, longing for your return; old age weighs heavy upon him.

" 'And this is how I sickened and died. The Archeress did not shoot me in my own house with those gentle shafts that never miss; it was no disease that made me pine away: but I missed you so much, and your clever wit and your gay merry ways, and life was sweet no longer, so I died.'

"When I heard this, I longed to throw my arms round her neck. Three times I tried to embrace the ghost, three times it slipt through my hands like a shadow or a dream. A sharp pang pierced my heart, and I cried out straight from my heart to hers:

" 'Mother dear! Why don't you stay with me when I long to embrace you? Let us relieve our hearts, and have a good cry in each other's arms. Are you only a phantom which awful Persephoneia has sent to make me more unhappy than ever?'

"My dear mother answered:

" 'Alas, alas, my child, most luckless creature on the face of the earth! Persephoneia is not deceiving you, she is the daughter of Zeus; but this is only what happens to mortals when one of us dies. As soon as the spirit leaves the white bones, the sinews no longer hold flesh and bones together— the blazing fire consumes them all; but the soul flits away fluttering like a dream. Make haste back to the light; but do not forget all this, tell it to your wife by and by.'

"As we were talking together, a crowd of women came up sent by awful Persephoneia, wives and daughters of great men. They gathered about the red blood, and I wondered how I should question them. This seemed to be the best plan. I drew my sword and kept off the crowd of ghosts; and then I let them form in a long line and come up one by one. Each one declared her lineage, then I questioned them all.

"Tryo came first, that noble dame. She said she was daughter of Salmoneus, and wife of Cretheus Aiolidês. . . .

"I saw the mother of Oidipûs, fair Epicastê, who did a monstrous thing in the innocence of her heart; for she married her own son, and he had slain his own father first. But the gods kept it from people's knowledge for a time. So he continued to be king in his lovely Thebes, but full of misery himself, by the god's cruel will; and she went down to the strong prison of Hadês the warder of the gates. Her grief was too great for her, and she hanged herself from a lofty roof-beam; but she left him misery enough and to spare, which the avenging spirit of his mother brought to pass.

"And I saw beautiful Chloris, whom Neleus married for her beauty, bringing magnificent gifts. She was the youngest daughter of Amphion Iasidês, the powerful King of Minyeian Orchomenos. She thus became Queen of Pylos, and bore him glorious sons, Nestor and Chromios and lordly Periclymenos. Besides these she was the mother of buxom Pero, the admiration of all beholders, wooed by every man within reach. But Neleus would give her to no man, unless he would carry off the cows of Iphiclês from Phylacê—a dangerous task! Iphiclês was a mighty man, the cows were well guarded, crumple-horned, broad-browed beauties. A certain admirable seer promised to drive them off all by himself, but hard fate caught him fast—there were the savage herdsmen and prison walls! Days and months went by, the year rolled round again and the seasons came back to their places, and then King Iphiclês let him go after he had uttered his oracles. So the will of Zeus came to pass.

"I saw Leda also, the wife of Tyndareos, who brought him two stout-hearted sons, Castor the horse-master and Polydeucês the great boxer. These two are both buried in mother earth, and both alive; even deep in the earth they have a special privilege from Zeus, one day living, and the next day dead, so they have the gods' own privilege.

"After her I saw Iphimedeia, the wife of Aloeus. . . . She bore him two sons, but they had only a short time to live. These were the famous Otos and Ephialtês, the biggest creatures the fruitful earth ever bred, and the most handsome next after famous Orion. At nine years old, they were nine cubits across the chest and nine fathoms high. They threatened to set up a horrible civil war against the immortals in Olympos. Their plan was to pile Ossa upon Olympos, and Pelion with its forests upon Ossa, and so to climb into heaven. Indeed they would have done it if they had lived to grow up; but they were killed by Apollo, the son of Zeus and Leto, before the down began to grow under their temples and the hair upon their chins.

"I saw Phaidra, and Procris, and fair Ariadnê, the daughter of grim-hearted Minos, whom Theseus carried off from Crete; he was taking her to Athenian soil, but he had no joy of her, for Artemis slew her first in the island of Dia because Dionysos told tales.

"Maira too I saw, and Clymenê, and accursed Eriphylê, who accepted gold as the price of her own husband. I will not stay to name all I saw, wives or daughters of heroes, or night would end before I had done. It is time to sleep now, either here or on board the ship; and to-morrow, please God, you will arrange for my homeward voyage."

When he had done, there was silence in the shadows of the hall, for they were all enchanted by the story. After a while Arêtê began to speak:

"What do you think of him now, gentlemen?" she said. "Isn't he a fine figure of a man, and clever enough for anything? Now he is *my* guest, but you all have your share of the honour, so don't be in a hurry to let him go, and don't stint your gifts which he needs so much. You have plenty of good things in store, thanks be to heaven."

Echeneos followed up, and said:

"My friends, what our wise queen says is not far from the mark; just what we might expect. You should do as she bids you. But here is Alcinoös, and all that we say or do depends on him."

Alcinoös answered at once:

"Well, this shall certainly be done, if I am still alive and king over the sea-faring Phaiacians. But let our guest make up his mind to stay at least over to-morrow, however anxious he may be to get home, and that will give me time to bring all our gifts together. To give him a safe journey is the concern of the whole nation, but mine most especially, since mine is the chief power in the land."

Odysseus answered readily:

"Most illustrious prince, if you should bid me to stay here for a twelvemonth, while you are making full preparations for the voyage and heaping your bounty upon me, that is just what I should choose: the fuller my hands, the better wel-

come I should find when I came home. They would all think
the more of me and love me better when they saw me in
Ithaca safe and sound."

To this Alcinoös replied:

"My dear Odysseus, to see you is quite enough to show
that you are no cheat or impostor, like so many others. There
is a rich crop of such men flourishing on the fat soil of this
world, who dress up fabulous tales about what no eye could
ever see. But there is the spirit of honest truth about your
story, as well as the artist's finish, and you have told it like a
poet who understands his craft. What a sad story of your own
travels and the whole Argive nation!

"But now be so kind as to tell us something more; did you
see any of your noble comrades who were at Ilion with you
and there met their fate? There is any amount of this long
night before us, it is not time for bed yet; please go on with
your tale of marvels. I could listen till daylight shall appear,
if you would have the patience to finish your touching story
under this roof."

Odysseus was ready to play up to him, and answered:

"Most illustrious prince, there is a time for long stories, and
there is a time for sleep; but if you wish to hear I would not
grudge you a story even more touching—the misfortunes of
those who perished afterwards, when they had come safe out
of the perils of the battlefield, and returned home only to fall
by the treachery of a woman.

"Very well, then. As soon as dread Persephoneia had dis-
persed the ghosts of the women, the ghost of Agamemnon
Atreidês came near full of sorrow: there was a crowd of
others round him, those who died with him in the house of
Aigisthos. The king knew me as soon as he had drunk the red
blood; he cried aloud and wept, stretching out his hands
towards me and trying to reach me. But there was no strength

or power left in him such as there used to be in that body so full of life. I shed tears of pity myself when I saw him, and spoke plainly as I called him by name:

" 'My lord Atreïdês, Agamemnon king of men! What fate of dolorous death brought you low? Did Poseidon raise a terrible tempest and drown you in the sea? Or did the hand of an enemy strike you down on dry land, in some foray or cattle-raid, or fighting for conquest and captives?'

"He answered, 'Prince Laertiadês, Odysseus ever ready! Poseidon did not drown me in the sea, no enemy struck me down on dry land; but Aigisthos plotted my death with my accursed wife—invited me to his house, set me down to a banquet, butchered me as if I were an ox at the manger! That was how I died, and a shameful death it was: my friends were falling, falling all round me, like a lot of tusker pigs that a rich man slaughters for a wedding or a banquet or a butty-meal! You have seen men fall in battle often enough, killed man to man or in the thick melée; but you never saw a sight so pitiable as that, as we lay about the winebowl, and the tables were piled with meats, and the floor running with blood.

" 'Most frightful of all was the shriek of Cassandra, and she a king's daughter! I heard it when the traitress Clytaimnestra killed her over my body. . . .

" 'True it is, there is nothing so cruel and shameless as a woman: that woman proved it to be true, when she plotted that shameful deed and murdered her lawful husband. Ah me, I did think to find welcome with my children and household when I came back to my home; but she had set her mind upon outrageous wickedness, she had brought shame on herself and all women for ever, even if one of them is honest.'

"I cried out:

" 'Mercy upon us! Indeed there is no doubt that Zeus

Allseeing has been the deadly foe of the house of Atreus
from the beginning, and he has always used the schemes of
women. For Helen's sake how many of us fell! and for you,
Clytaimnestra was laying her plot while you were far away!'

"He answered:

" 'Then take warning now yourself, and never be too kind
even to your wife. Never tell her all you have in your mind;
you may tell something, but keep something to yourself.
However, *you* will not be murdered by your wife, Odysseus.
She is full of intelligence, and her heart is sound, your
prudent and modest Penelopeia.

" 'Ah, she was a young bride when we left her and went to
the war; there was a baby boy at her breast, and I suppose by
this time he counts himself a man. Happy boy! His father will
see him when he comes, sure enough, and he will give his
father a kiss as a good boy should. But my wife would not
even let me delight my eyes with the sight of my son; she
killed the father first.

" 'But there is something I want very much to know. Have
you heard anything about my son's being alive somewhere
in Orchomenos, or in sandy Pylos, or perhaps with Menelaos
in Sparta? My Orestês is certainly not dead yet.'

"I said, 'Why do you ask me that, Atreïdês? I know
nothing, whether he is alive or dead; and it is a bad thing to
babble like the blowing wind.'

"As we two stood talking together of our sorrows in this
mournful way, other ghosts came up: Achillês and Pa-
troclos, and Antilochos, the man without stain and without
reproach, and Aias, who was most handsome and noble of
all next to the admirable Achillês. The ghost of Achillês
knew me, and said in plain words:

" 'Here is Prince Odysseus who never fails! O you fool-
hardy man! Your ingenious brain will never do better than

this. How did you dare to come down to Hadês, where dwell the dead without sense or feeling, phantoms of mortals whose weary days are done?'

"I answered him, 'My lord Achillês Peleïdês, our chief and our champion before Troy! I came to ask Teiresias if he had any advice or help for me on my way to my rugged island home. For I have not yet set foot in my own country, since trouble has ever been my lot. But you, Achillês, are most blessed of all men who ever were or will be. When you lived, we honoured you like the gods; and now you are a potentate in this world of the dead. Then do not deplore your death, Achillês.'

"He answered at once, 'Don't bepraise death to me, Odysseus. I would rather be plowman to a yeoman farmer on a small holding than lord Paramount in the kingdom of the dead.

" 'But do tell me something about that fine son of mine. Did he go to the war and take a leading place, or not? And tell me of my noble old father—have you heard anything of Peleus? Does he still hold his honourable place among the Myrmidons, or have they lost respect for him throughout the land because his hands and feet are stiff with age? For I am no longer under the sun to help him, strong as I once was on the battlefield of Troy, when I struck down the best of them and defended our people. Let me be for a short time in my father's house strong as I once was, and I would make not a few fear my anger and my invincible hands, if they are keeping him by force from his honour due!'

"I answered, 'I have nothing to tell you of your noble father Peleus, but I can tell you about your beloved son Neoptolemos, and there is nothing to hide. In fact I brought him in my own ship from Scyros to join the Achaian army. When we held a council of war, he was always the first to speak, and always found the right thing to say. Only Nestor and I were superior. When we met our enemies in battle, he did not lag among the crowd or in the scrimmage, but showed himself well in front, the bravest of the brave: many a man he killed in fair fight.

" 'I will not name all those he killed on the field, but what a man was brought low when he ran his sword through Eurypylos Telephidês, that young hero! and many others of his people fell by his side that a woman might enjoy her gewgaws! That was the handsomest man I ever saw, except Memnon the magnificent. And when the best men of our army were about to enter the Wooden Horse which Epeios made, and I was put in charge to open and close the door as I thought fit, the other captains were wiping tears from their eyes and trembling in every limb, but I saw no pallor on his cheeks and no tear in his eyes. Again and again he begged me to let him out, and handled his sword-hilt and heavy spear, eager to have at his enemies.

" 'When at last we had sacked the city, he took his share of the spoil and a special prize, and embarked unwounded, with never a scratch from sword or spear, although there are plenty of those in war. You take your luck when war runs amuck.'

"When I told him this, the ghost of clean-heeled Achillês marched away with long steps over the meadow of asphodel, proud to hear how his son had made his mark.

"The other ghosts of the dead halted in turn, and each asked what was near to his heart; but alone of them all the soul of Aias Telamoniadês kept apart, still resentful for my victory over him when there was question about the arms of Achillês. The goddess his mother set them up as a prize for the best man. How I wish I had never won such a prize! What a life was lost for that! Aias, first of all the Danaäns in noble looks and noble deeds, except Achillês the incomparable. And so I addressed him in gentle words:

" 'Aias, great son of a great father! were you never to forget your anger against me for those accursed arms, not even in death? That prize was a disaster, seeing that we lost a tower of strength like you. Our whole nation mourns your loss continually, no less than we mourn Achillês Peleïadês. Zeus alone is to blame and no one else, because he hated the Danaän host so vehemently, and brought fate upon you. Nay, come this way, my lord, and listen to my pleading: master your passion and your proud temper.'

"He replied not a word, but moved away into Erebos after the other ghosts of the dead. Then in spite of all, he should have spoken to me, or I to him; but I wished to see the souls of the others who were dead.

"There I saw Minos the glorious son of Zeus, holding a golden rod and giving sentence upon the dead. He was seated, and the dead were around him in the house of Hadês with its wide portals, some seated and some standing, as each asked the judge for his decision.

"After him I noticed the huge figure of Orion driving the beasts in a mass over the meadow of asphodel, the game which he had killed himself when he was alive on the lonely hills; his hands held a cudgel of solid bronze, unbroken for ever.

"And I saw Tityos the son of Gaia most majestic, lying upon the ground; nine roods he covered, and two vultures sat, one on each side, and tore his liver, plunging under the skin: he could not defend himself with his hands. This was his punishment because he had laid violent hands on Leto, the famous consort of Zeus, when she was passing through the beautiful grounds of Panopeus on her way to Pytho.

"Tantalos also I saw in his misery, standing in a lake up to his chin, always thirsty, but try as he would, not a drop could he lap up: for as often as the poor old man dipt his head to take a drink, the water was sucked back and disappeared, until the dark earth showed under his feet as fate dried it away. Tall trees in full leaf dangled their fruit over his head, pears and pomegranates and fine juicy apples, sweet figs and ripe olives; but as often as the poor old man reached out a hand to catch one, the wind tossed them all up to the clouds.

"Sisyphos also I saw and his tedious task, as he held up a monstrous stone with both hands. Scrambling with his feet, and pushing with his hands, he heaved the stone up the hill; but just as he was about to topple it over the crest, the weight was too much for him, and turned it back: down-along to the ground rolled the stone pitiless. Then he would push again, stretching and struggling, with sweat pouring off every limb and the dust rising from his head.

"After him I saw mighty Heraclês, his phantom that is: but Heraclês himself is with the immortal gods, as happy as the day is long, with graceful Youth for his bride. Around this phantom the ghosts were gibbering and twittering like a flock of birds, and scattering hither and thither; he stood holding his naked bow with arrow on string, looking as black as night, and casting dreadful glances round, for ever as if just about to shoot. A terrible baldric was round about his chest, a golden strap covered with wonderful work, bears and wild boars and glaring lions, battles and conflicts and bloody death. May the artist never invent another work of art who made that terrible baldric by his genius! The hero knew me when he caught sight of me, and sped his words straight to the mark:

" 'Prince Laërtiadês, Odysseus never failing! I pity you, for you are dogged by an evil fate, as I was, under the light of the sun! My father was Zeus Cronion, yet I had infinite tribulation to endure; for I was bound to a contemptible fellow who set me dangerous labours. Once he sent me here for the Dog, because he thought he could find no more dangerous labour than that. I brought him up, I got him from Hadês sure enough, under conduct of Hermeias and Pallas Athena.'

"With these words he strode back into the house of Hadês; but I remained where I was, in case any other of the heroes of past times should appear. And indeed, I should have seen others of those ancient men whom I wished especially to see, as Theseus and Peirithoös, those famous sons of gods; but before I could see them, the innumerable hosts of the dead gathered together with deafening cries, and I grew pale with fear that awful Persephoneia might send out of Hadês upon me a Gorgon-head of some dreadful monster. Then I went back at once to the ship, and told my men to loose the hawser and get away. They were soon rowing steadily on their benches, and the current bore us steadily down the ocean stream; oars at first, afterwards a following breeze.

BOOK XII

THE SINGING SIRENS, AND THE TERRORS OF
SCYLLA AND CHARYBDIS

"Our ship left the stream of Oceano, and passed into the open sea. Soon it came to the island of Aiaia, where Dawn has her dwelling and her dancing lawns, and Helios his place of rising. We ran up the ship, and went ashore to sleep on the beach.

"As soon as the next day dawned, I sent my companions to Circê's house to bring the body of Elpenor. We cut chunks of wood for a pyre, and buried him on the end of the foreland, mourning for our dead friend. And when the body was burnt with his arms, we raised a barrow with a large stone upon it and set up his own oar on the summit.

"While we were busy there, Circê did not fail to learn that we had come back from Hadês. She soon came down well provided; the servants brought a load of bread and meat and sparkling red wine. Then standing among us, she said:

" 'You men stick at nothing! So you went down to Hadês alive? Double-diers, when other people are content to die once! Come now, eat and drink once more, all the day is before you; and to-morrow at dawn you shall sail. I will describe the way, I will tell you every single thing, that you may not make mischief for yourselves and come to grief by land or sea.'

"We were quite ready to comply. So all the day long till sunset we enjoyed our feast of good things. When the sun set and darkness came, they all lay down where the ship was moored; but Circê took me apart, and made me tell the story of our voyage as we sat together. I told her everything just as it happened, and at the end she said:

" 'Very well, all that is finished and done with. Now listen to what I have to say, and you will not forget it, please God.

" 'First you will come to the Sirens, who bewitch every one who comes near them. If any man draws near in his innocence and listens to their voice, he never sees home again, never again will wife and little children run to greet him with joy; but the Sirens bewitch him with their melodious song. There in a meadow they sit, and all round is a great heap of bones, mouldering bodies and withering skins. Go on past that place, and do not let the men hear; you must knead a good lump of wax and plug their ears with pellets. If you wish to hear them yourself, make the men tie up your hands and feet and fasten your body tight to the mast, and then you can enjoy the song as much as you like. Tell them that if you shout out and command them to let you loose, they must tie you tighter with a few more ropes.

" 'When you have got clear of them, there is a choice of two courses, and I will not lay down for you which to take; use your own judgment. I will just say what they are. One course will bring you to a pair of precipitous rocks, washed by the boisterous breakers of dark-eyed Amphitritê; the gods call them the Moving Rocks. Not a bird can pass between them, not even the timorous doves which carry the ambrosia to Father Zeus; one of these is always caught between the towering rocks, and the Father sends in another to keep the number right. No ship sailed by men that came that way has ever escaped, but timbers and dead bodies are all carried away by the rolling seas and tempests of blazing fire. Only one ship ever sailed through, the well-known *Argo,* on her voyage to Aiëtas; and she also would have been wrecked

on the rocks, but Hera took her safely through because
Jason was her friend.

" 'The other course leads between two cliffs. One drives a
sharp peak high into the heavens, and black clouds are
round about it; the clouds never disperse, and that peak is
never clear either in summer or in autumn. No mortal man
could climb up, no man climb down, not if he had twenty
hands and twenty feet; for the stone is smooth as if it had
been polished. But in the side of the cliff is a dark gloomy
cave, facing the west towards Erebos, just where you will
steer your ship, Odysseus. There Scylla dwells, and yelps in
her dreadful way; the cave is so high that the strongest man
could not reach it with an arrow shot from the ship. It is true
her voice is no louder than a puppy-dog new-born, but she is
a horrible monster! Such a sight could give pleasure to no
one, not even one of the immortal gods. She has twelve
flapping feet, and six necks enormously long, and at the end
of each neck a horrible head with three rows of teeth set
thick and close, full of black death. She is hidden in the cave
as far as the waist, but she pokes out her heads from the
gloomy depths; and there she fishes, hunting all round for
dolphins and swordfish, or any of those leviathans of the
deep which Amphitritê breeds in thousands. No seamen
can boast that they have escaped scot-free from her: she
grabs a poor wretch with each head out of the ship as it
sails along.

" 'The other cliff is lower, as you will see, Odysseus. They
are not far from one another; you could shoot an arrow
across. There is a wild fig-tree growing from it, a tall tree
covered with leaves; and Charybdis underneath swallows
down the black water. Three times a day she spouts it out,
three times a day she swallows it down: she is a terror—
don't you be there when she swallows! No one could save

you from destruction, not Earthshaker himself! You had much better go by Scylla's rock, keep close, and be quick about it. To lose six of your crew is much better than to lose them all at once!'

"I answered, 'What do you say to this, my goddess—Suppose I slip away from Charybdis, and show fight when the other attacks my men?'

"She answered at once, 'You hot-head! fighting and asking for trouble is all you care about! Will you stand up even to the immortal gods? She is no mortal, I tell you, but an immortal fiend, dangerous, deadly, savage, invincible! There is no help for it; flight is better than fight. If you stay too long near the rock while you put on your armour, I am afraid she may shoot out another half-dozen heads and catch another half-dozen fellows! No, no, row as hard as you can, and call for help on Crataiïs—that is Scylla's mother, she produced that abomination! Crataiïs will stop her from trying again.

" 'You will come next to the island of Thrinacia, where the herds of Helios feed. There are his cattle and great sheep, seven herds of cattle and seven fine flocks of sheep, fifty in each. These never have young, and never die. Their shepherds are two goddesses, nymphs with lovely hair, shining Phaëthusa and bright Lampetiê, daughters of Helios Hyperion by divine Neaira ever young. When the mother had brought up her children, she sent them away to that far-off island, to look after their father's cattle and sheep. If you leave these unharmed and attend to the business of getting home, you may yet reach Ithaca, although not without suffering; but if you do any damage, then I foretell destruction for ship and men. You may save your own life, but if you do, you will reach your home late and miserable, and all your companions will be lost.'

"As she said these words, the Dawn rose enthroned in gold. Circê went away up the island; and I to the ship, where I awakened my companions, and bade them embark and cast off the moorings. They were soon on board and in their places. Circê our beautiful goddess, who could speak to us men in our own language, sent us the best of companions, a fair wind to fill our sails: all was snug and ship-shape, we sat still and let the wind carry us on while the steersman kept the course.

"I was anxious enough, of course, and so I spoke to the men. 'My friends, the divine Circê has told me all about what is going to happen; and I do not think it right that only one or two should know, so I will tell you all, and when we all know, we may die or escape as the case may be. First, she bids us keep away from the Sirens with their wonderful voices and their flowery meadow. I alone must hear them, so she said; but you are to bind me with strong ropes and fasten me upright against the mast, so that I shall not be able to move. If I implore you and order you to set me free, you must tie me up tighter than ever.'

"So I explained everything to my companions; and by this time the ship was drawing near to the Sirens' isle, travelling briskly, for there was no fault to be found with the wind. Then the wind fell all at once, and there was a dead calm, not a ripple on the water. My men rolled up the sail and stowed it below, and they were soon rowing away, white foam and splashing oars. Then I took a thick round of wax, and chopt it up with my sword into pellets, and moulded the bits in my fingers. The wax grew soft, as it was warmed by the effulgence of my lord Helios Hyperionidês, and I plugged up the ears of all the men one after another. Then they bound me hand and foot and fastened me upright against the mast, took their places and paddled on. But when she was as far off the land as a voice could carry, and going at a good pace, the Sirens saw us coming and raised their melodious song:

" 'Come this way, most admirable Odysseus, glory of the nation! stay your ship, and listen to our voice! No man ever yet sailed past this place, without first listening to the voice which sounds from our lips sweet as honey! No, he has a great treat and goes home a wiser man. For we know all that the Argives and Trojans endured on the plains before Troy by the will of Heaven; and we know all that shall come to pass on the face of mother earth!'

"So they sang in lovely tones. From the bottom of my heart I longed to listen, and I ordered the men to set me free, nodding my head and working my brows; but they simply went on pulling with a good swing. Perimedês and Eury-lochos at once got up, and put more ropes round me and fastened me tighter. But when we had gone a long way past the Sirens, so that we could hear them no longer, my companions took out the wax from their ears and untied my ropes.

"At last we left the island behind; and suddenly I saw smoke, and a great rolling wave, and heard a loud noise. The men were terrified, the oars flew out of their hands and fell in the sea with a splash, dragging down at the ship's sides by their loops; she made no way, now the oars drove no longer. I walked down the whole length of the ship, pausing by each man, and coaxing them not to lose heart:

" 'My friends, we are not unacquainted with trouble. This is no greater danger than when the Cyclops imprisoned us in his cave by brute force; we escaped from that place, thanks to my courage and my ingenious plan, and I think we shall live to remember this no less. Now then, attend to my instructions. Keep your seats and row away like men, and then we may hope that Zeus will save and deliver us out of

this danger. Now for you, steersman, pay careful heed, for
you hold our helm in your hands. Keep her well away from
the smoke and surge, and hug the cliffs; whatever you do,
don't let her run off in that direction, or we shall all be
drowned.'

"They did my bidding at once. But I took care not to men-
tion Scylla and the peril we could not avoid; I thought they
would be likely to leave the oars in a panic and huddle down
below. At that moment I quite forgot Circê's injunction,
when she told me not to arm myself. I put on my armour,
and caught up a couple of spears, and took my stand on the
foredeck; for that was where I thought Scylla would show
herself on the rock, bringing death for my companions. But I
could not see her anywhere, though I dazed my eyes with
staring about me through the clouds at the rock.

"We passed up the strait, groaning loudly; for on one side
was Scylla, on the other Charybdis swallowed up the salt
water in terrible fashion. When she spouted, like a cauldron
over a great fire she seethed up in a swirling mess, and the
spray rose high in the air till it fell on the tops of the two
cliffs: when she swallowed up the salt sea, she showed deep
down in her swirling whirlpool black sand at the bottom, and
the rocks all round echoed a bellowing boom. Every man was
pale with fear. As we gazed in our fear at the death on this
side, at the same moment Scylla grabbed six of my men out of
the ship, the best and strongest of the crew. I turned, took a
glance at the ship, looked for my men, saw their hands and
feet already in the air swinging aloft in the clutches of Scylla;
while they called aloud on my name, for the last time, in
despair. As a fisherman stands on a projecting rock with a
long rod, and throws in ground-bait to attract the little
fishes, then drops in hook and line with its horn-bait, and at
last gets a bite and whips him out gasping, so Scylla swung

them gasping up to the rock; there in the cave she devoured them, shrieking and stretching out their hands to me in the death-struggle. That was the most pitiable sight my eyes ever beheld in all my toils and troubles on the weary ways of the sea.

"When we were past the rocks, and away from the terrors of Charybdis and Scylla, immediately we reached a delectable island; in that place were the fine cattle with broad brows and the great sheep which belonged to Helios Hyperion. While we were still a long way off I heard the lowing of the cattle penned for the night, and the bleating of sheep; and I remembered the warning of the blind prophet, Theban Teiresias, and of Aiaian Circê, and how they strictly forbade me to land on the island of Helios the joy of man. At once I said to my companions, with my mind full of foreboding:

" 'Men, you are having a hard time of it, I know that, but listen to me a moment; I want to tell you a warning of Teiresias and of Circê also. They strictly forbade us to land on the island of Helios; for there they said an awful danger awaits us. You had better give the island a wide berth and row on.'

"This fairly broke them down, and Eurylochos answered at once angrily:

" 'You are a hard man, Odysseus, never downhearted and never tired! You must be made of iron! Here are your men, tired to death and scarce able to keep awake, and you won't let us go ashore on this island and cook a square meal. No, you make us go trapesing along the whole blessed night. We must give the island a wide berth and toss about in the dark! Night is the time for dangerous squalls, that's the way ships are lost! How can we expect to get off with our lives if a sudden squall comes out of the south or west? Damned bad winds, that send a ship to the bottom, God willing or not! I vote we take our orders from black Madam Night, pull up the vessel and cook a meal. Then in the morning in we get, and it's over the sea we go!'

"That was the proposal of Eurylochos, and the others applauded. Then I understood that heaven had trouble in store for us, and I gave it him straight:

" 'Eurylochos, I must give way to force. I am one against many. But you must swear a solemn oath, that if we find a herd of cattle or a flock of sheep no one shall dare to kill one cow or one sheep. You must keep quiet, and eat the food that Circê gave us.'

"They all swore the oath accordingly; and when that business was done, we brought the ship into a land-locked harbour close to a spring of sweet water. They all went ashore, and prepared their meal in proper style. When they had taken all they wanted, they had time to remember their lost comrades, whom Scylla had caught and eaten out of the ship; and they lamented their dead until welcome sleep overcame them. But when it was the third watch of the night and the stars had moved south, Zeus Cloudgatherer sent out a furious wind in a regular tempest, and covered earth and sea with clouds; night rushed down from the heavens. As soon as the dawn showed ruddy through the mist, we hauled the ship ashore into a cave, in which the Nymphs had their thrones and dancing-rings. Then I called the men together and addressed them:

" 'My friends, we have food and drink in the ship, so we must keep our hands off these cattle or we may suffer for it. For an awful god is the owner of these cattle and great sheep—Helios, who sees all and hears all.'

"They were quite willing to agree. But the south wind blew for a whole month without changing, and after that, never a breath of any wind we had but east and south. So

long as the food and red wine lasted, they kept their hands
off the cattle, for they did not want to die; but when all the
provisions on board were consumed, and they had to go
about hunting for game, birds, or fish, or whatever fell to
their hands or their hooks, and they were half starved, I
made my way up into the island to offer prayer to the gods
and try whether one would help us. I slipt away from the
men and found a place with shelter from the wind; there I
washed my hands, and prayed to all the gods who dwell in
Olympos, but they made me fall into a deep sleep.

"Meanwhile Eurylochos was making a fatal speech to
his companions. 'My friends,' he said, 'you are in a bad
way; but let me say a word to you. All deaths are hateful to
miserable mortals, but the most pitiable death of all is to
starve. Come along, let us drive off the best of these cattle,
and sacrifice them to the immortal gods who rule the broad
heavens. If we ever return home to Ithaca, we will build a
rich temple to Helios Hyperion, and set up there many
handsome offerings; but if the god is angry about his straight-
horns, and wants to destroy our ship, and if the other gods
agree, I choose rather to die once with a mouthful of salt
water than to be slowly squeezed out in a desert island.'

"The others applauded this speech. They wasted no time,
but drove off the best of the cattle of Helios close by, for the
fine beasts with their wide foreheads and crumpled horns
used to graze not far off. The men stood round the cattle and
prayed to the gods, but they had no barley-meal to sprinkle
upon their victims, so they used tender young oak-leaves
which they picked from a tree. They had no wine to pour
over the burnt offering, but they sprinkled water before they
cooked the tripes. Then they chopt up the rest and put the
pieces on spits.

"At that moment I awoke and came back to the seashore.

As I came near to the ship a sweetish odour of burning fat was diffused around me. I cried aloud in horror and prayed to the immortal gods:

" 'Father Zeus, and all ye blessed gods that live for ever! You meant my ruin when ye made me fall into that cruel sleep! My men whom I left behind have committed a monstrous crime!'

"A messenger took the news quickly to Helios Hyperion, Lampetiê in her flowing robe, and she told him we had slain his cattle. In great anger he called out to the immortals:

" 'Father Zeus and all ye gods that live for ever! Punish those men of Odysseus Laërtiadês! They have brutally killed my cattle, which were my great delight when I climbed into the starry sky, and when I turned back to earth from heaven. If they do not pay me a fitting compensation, I will just go down to Hadês and show my light among the dead!'

"Zeus Cloudgatherer answered him, 'Now then, Helios, you just go on showing your light to us immortals and to mortal men upon mother earth. I will soon strike the ship with a thunderbolt, and smash it into smithereens in the middle of the sea!'

"I was told this later by Calypso; she said she heard it herself from Hermês King's Messenger.

"As soon as I came down to the seashore, I reproached them one and all, though we could do nothing to help it now: the cattle were already dead. But awful portents were seen in that place: the skins crawled, the meat bellowed on the spits, both raw and roast; it was like the noise of cattle.

"Six days my companions feasted on the best of the cattle of Helios; but when the seventh day came, the furious tempest ceased; we embarked and went sailing away over the sea.

"When the island was far astern and no other land to be

seen, nothing but sea and sky, Cronion brought a black cloud over our ship and darkened the deep. Then she did not run long, for suddenly came the west wind screeching and blowing with a furious tempest, the gale broke both the forestays, the mast fell aft, and all the tackle tumbled into the hold, the mast hit the steersman's head and crushed the skull to splinters, he took a header from his deck and was drowned. Zeus at the same time thundered and struck our ship with his bolt; she shivered in all her timbers at the blow, and the place was full of sulphur. The men were cast out, there they were bobbing up and down on the waves like so many crows. So God ended the homeward voyage for them.

"I kept pacing up and down the ship, until the sea tore the sides from the keel. A rolling wave carried her along dismantled, and snapt off the mast close to the keel, but the backstay had fallen upon it; this was made of stout oxhide, so I used it to lash together keel and mast, and I rode upon these drifting before those terrible winds.

"Now the furious tempest of the west wind was lulled, and the south quickly followed, bringing anxiety for me, for it was sure to carry me back again to the terrors of Charybdis. All night long I drifted, and by sunrise Scylla and dreadful Charybdis were before me. Charybdis swallowed up the salt water; but I had been carried high up, and caught the wild fig-tree; and I stuck to it like a bat and held tight. I had nothing to plant my feet upon for support and no way to climb; for the roots were far below, and the branches far above, those thick long branches which overshadowed Charybdis. But I held tight without slackening until my mast and keel should be spouted up again. How I longed for them! and they came at last. At the time when a judge gets up from court for his dinner, after settling the morning's disputes among quarrelsome young men, just at that time my spars appeared out of Charybdis. I spread out hands and feet and let go, and came down plump in the water alongside the spars, and then clambered up and lay on them, paddling with my hands. What of Scylla? The Father of gods and men would not allow her to set eyes on me, or I should not have escaped with my life.

"From that place I drifted for nine days, and on the tenth at night the gods brought me to the island of Ogygia. There dwells Calypso, that goddess so beautiful and so terrible, who can speak the language of man; and she cared for me. But why go on with my story? I have told it already, and no one cares for a twice-told tale."

ARISTOTLE was born in 384 B.C. in Stagira, a Greek colonial town on the Aegean. At the age of seventeen he entered the Academy in Athens conducted by Plato. He remained at the school until Plato's death, twenty years later. For a period of seven years he tutored Alexander, the future conqueror of much of Asia, and then returned to Athens to found his own school in the Lyceum. His habit of lecturing while walking gave his school the name "Peripatetic." The treatises of Aristotle were probably originally prepared as lectures or reading assignments for his students. Aristotle's interests changed as he grew older. His early work was concerned mainly with logic and metaphysics. In his later life he became more absorbed in the study of nature, politics, and literature. In 323 B.C. Aristotle left Athens because of rising political agitation and fled to Chalcis, where he died in 322 B.C.

LUCIUS ANNAEUS SENECA was born in Spain about 3 B.C. His promising legal career was interrupted when in A.D. 41, on the instigation of an enemy, he was exiled by the Emperor Claudius. Eight years later he was recalled to become tutor to the young Nero. In the first years of Nero's rule Seneca exerted a beneficial influence on the emperor. After amassing a huge fortune, Seneca retired from public life and was rarely seen in Rome. He had made powerful enemies, however, some of whom influenced Nero against him. On a charge of complicity in a conspiracy, Nero forced him to end his life in A.D. 65. As Tacitus relates: "He turned to his friends and said that, since he was prevented from rewarding their services, he would leave to them the one thing, and yet the best thing, that he had to leave—the pattern of his life." The surviving writings of Seneca include a number of moral essays, nine tragedies, and the letters, of which "How Many 'Causes'?" and "The Sole Good" are examples. The letters are regarded, with those of Cicero and Pliny, as the best to come down from antiquity.

ARISTOTLE
Rhetoric
SELECTIONS

LUCIUS ANNAEUS SENECA
How Many "Causes"?
The Sole Good

NUMBER **2**
SET FIVE

THE GREAT BOOKS FOUNDATION   *Chicago*

From RHETORIC, *Aristotle. Translated by W. Rhys Roberts.*
By permission of the Clarendon Press, Oxford.

From THE STOIC PHILOSOPHY OF SENECA *translated by*
Moses Hadas. Copyright © 1958 by Moses Hadas.
Reprinted by permission of Doubleday & Company, Inc.

The special contents of this edition are copyright 1963
by THE GREAT BOOKS FOUNDATION.

Printed in the United States of America.

published and distributed by

THE GREAT BOOKS FOUNDATION
a non-profit corporation
5 South Wabash Avenue, Chicago 3, Illinois

BOOK I, CHAPTER 5

IT MAY BE said that every individual man and all men in common aim at a certain end which determines what they choose and what they avoid. This end, to sum it up briefly, is happiness and its constituents. Let us, then, by way of illustration only, ascertain what is in general the nature of happiness, and what are the elements of its constituent parts. For all advice to do things or not to do them is concerned with happiness and with the things that make for or against it; whatever creates or increases happiness or some part of happiness, we ought to do; whatever destroys or hampers happiness, or gives rise to its opposite, we ought not to do.

We may define happiness as prosperity combined with virtue; or as independence of life; or as the secure enjoyment of the maximum of pleasure; or as a good condition of property and body, together with the power of guarding one's property and body and making use of them. That happiness is one or more of these things, pretty well everybody agrees.

From this definition of happiness it follows that its constituent parts are:—good birth, plenty of friends, good friends, wealth, good children, plenty of children, a happy old age, also such bodily excellences as health, beauty, strength, large stature, athletic powers, together with fame, honour, good luck, and virtue. A man cannot fail to be completely independent if he possesses these internal and these external goods; for besides these there are no others

1

to have. (Goods of the soul and of the body are internal. Good birth, friends, money, and honour are external.) Further, we think that he should possess resources and luck, in order to make his life really secure. As we have already ascertained what happiness in general is, so now let us try to ascertain what each of these parts of it is.

Now good birth in a race or a state means that its members are indigenous or ancient; that its earliest leaders were distinguished men, and that from them have sprung many who were distinguished for qualities that we admire.

The good birth of an individual, which may come either from the male or the female side, implies that both parents are free citizens, and that, as in the case of the state, the founders of the line have been notable for virtue or wealth or something else which is highly prized, and that many distinguished persons belong to the family, men and women, young and old.

The phrases 'possession of good children' and 'of many children' bear a quite clear meaning. Applied to a community, they mean that its young men are numerous and of good quality: good in regard to bodily excellences, such as stature, beauty, strength, athletic powers; and also in regard to the excellences of the soul, which in a young man are temperance and courage. Applied to an individual, they mean that his own children are numerous and have the good qualities we have described. Both male and female are here included; the excellences of the latter are, in body, beauty and stature; in soul, self-command and an industry that is not sordid. Communities as well as individuals should lack none of these perfections, in their women as well as in their men. Where, as among the Lacedaemonians, the state of women is bad, almost half of human life is spoilt.

The constituents of wealth are: plenty of coined money

and territory; the ownership of numerous, large, and beautiful estates; also the ownership of numerous and beautiful implements, live stock, and slaves. All these kinds of property are our own, are secure, gentlemanly, and useful. The useful kinds are those that are productive, the gentlemanly kinds are those that provide enjoyment. By 'productive' I mean those from which we get our income; by 'enjoyable', those from which we get nothing worth mentioning except the use of them. The criterion of 'security' is the ownership of property in such places and under such conditions that the use of it is in our power; and it is 'our own' if it is in our own power to dispose of it or keep it. By 'disposing of it' I mean giving it away or selling it. Wealth as a whole consists in using things rather than in owning them; it is really the activity—that is, the use—of property that constitutes wealth.

Fame means being respected by everybody, or having some quality that is desired by all men, or by most, or by the good, or by the wise.

Honour is the token of a man's being famous for doing good. It is chiefly and most properly paid to those who have already done good; but also to the man who can do good in future. Doing good refers either to the preservation of life and the means of life, or to wealth, or to some other of the good things which it is hard to get either always or at that particular place or time—for many gain honour for things which seem small, but the place and the occasion account for it. The constituents of honour are: sacrifices; commemoration, in verse or prose; privileges; grants of land; front seats at civic celebrations; state burial; statues; public maintenance; among foreigners, obeisances and giving place; and such presents as are among various bodies of men regarded as marks of honour. For a present is not only the bestowal of a piece of property, but also a token of honour; which explains why honour-loving as well as money-loving persons desire it. The present brings to both what they want; it is a piece of property, which is what the lovers of money desire; and it brings honour, which is what the lovers of honour desire.

The excellence of the body is health; that is, a condition which allows us, while keeping free from disease, to have the use of our bodies; for many people are 'healthy' as we are told Herodicus was; and these no one can congratulate on their 'health', for they have to abstain from everything or nearly everything that men do.—Beauty varies with the time of life. In a young man beauty is the possession of a body fit to endure the exertion of running and of contests of strength; which means that he is pleasant to look at; and therefore all-round athletes are the most beautiful, being naturally adapted both for contests of strength and for speed also. For a man in his prime, beauty is fitness for the exertion of warfare, together with a pleasant but at the same time formidable appearance. For an old man, it is to be strong enough for such exertion as is necessary, and to be free from all those deformities of old age which cause pain to others. Strength is the power of moving some one else at will; to do this, you must either pull, push, lift, pin, or grip him; thus you must be strong in all of those ways or at least in some. Excellence in size is to surpass ordinary people in height, thickness, and breadth by just as much as will not make one's movements slower in consequence. Athletic excellence of the body consists in size, strength, and swiftness; swiftness implying strength. He who can fling forward his legs in a certain way, and move them fast and far, is good at running; he who can grip and hold down is good at wrestling; he who can drive an adversary from his ground with the right blow is a good boxer: he who can do both the last is a good pancratiast, while he who can do all is an 'all-round' athlete.

Happiness in old age is the coming of old age slowly and painlessly; for a man has not this happiness if he grows old either quickly, or tardily but painfully. It arises both from the excellences of the body and from good luck. If a man is not free from disease, or if he is not strong, he will not be free from suffering; nor can he continue to live a long and painless life unless he has good luck. There is, indeed, a capacity for long life that is quite independent of health or strength; for many people live long who lack the excellences of the body; but for our present purpose there is no use in going into the details of this.

The terms 'possession of many friends' and 'possession of good friends' need no explanation; for we define a 'friend' as one who will always try, for your sake, to do what he takes to be good for you. The man towards whom many feel thus has many friends; if these are worthy men, he has good friends.

'Good luck' means the acquisition or possession of all or most, or the most important, of those good things which are due to luck. Some of the things that are due to luck may also be due to artificial contrivance; but many are independent of art, as for example those which are due to nature—though, to be sure, things due to luck may actually be contrary to nature. Thus health may be due to artificial contrivance, but beauty and stature are due to nature. All such good things as excite envy are, as a class, the outcome of good luck. Luck is also the cause of good things that happen contrary to reasonable expectation: as when, for instance, all your brothers are ugly, but you are handsome yourself; or when you find a treasure that everybody else has overlooked; or when a missile hits the next man and misses you;

or when you are the only man not to go to a place you have gone to regularly, while the others go there for the first time and are killed. All such things are reckoned pieces of good luck.

As to virtue, it is most closely connected with the subject of Eulogy, and therefore we will wait to define it until we come to discuss that subject.

We have now to consider Virtue and Vice, the Noble and the Base, since these are the objects of praise and blame. In doing so, we shall at the same time be finding out how to make our hearers take the required view of our own characters—our second method of persuasion. The ways in which to make them trust the goodness of other people are also the ways in which to make them trust our own. Praise, again, may be serious or frivolous; nor is it always of a human or divine being but often of inanimate things, or of the humblest of the lower animals. Here too we must know on what grounds to argue, and must, therefore, now discuss the subject, though by way of illustration only.

The Noble is that which is both desirable for its own sake and also worthy of praise; or that which is both good and also pleasant because good. If this is a true definition of the Noble, it follows that virtue must be noble, since it is both a good thing and also praiseworthy. Virtue is, according to the usual view, a faculty of providing and preserving good things; or a faculty of conferring many great benefits, and benefits of all kinds on all occasions. The forms of Virtue are justice, courage, temperance, magnificence, magnanimity, liberality, gentleness, prudence, wisdom. If virtue is a faculty of beneficence, the highest kinds of it must be those which are most useful to others, and for this reason men honour most the just and the courageous, since courage is useful to others in war, justice both in war and in peace. Next comes liberality; liberal people let their money go instead of fighting for it, whereas other people care more for money than for anything else. Justice is the virtue through which everybody enjoys his

7

own possessions in accordance with the law; its opposite is in-justice, through which men enjoy the possessions of others in defiance of the law. Courage is the virtue that disposes men to do noble deeds in situations of danger, in accordance with the law and in obedience to its commands; cowardice is the opposite. Temperance is the virtue that disposes us to obey the law where physical pleasures are concerned; incontinence is the opposite. Liberality disposes us to spend money for others' good; illiberality is the opposite. Magnanimity is the virtue that disposes us to do good to others on a large scale; [its opposite is meanness of spirit]. Magnificence is a virtue productive of greatness in matters involving the spend-ing of money. The opposites of these two are smallness of spirit and meanness respectively. Prudence is that virtue of the understanding which enables men to come to wise decisions about the relation to happiness of the goods and evils that have been previously mentioned.

The above is a sufficient account, for our present purpose, of virtue and vice in general, and of their various forms. As to further aspects of the subject, it is not difficult to discern the facts; it is evident that things productive of virtue are noble, as tending towards virtue; and also the effects of vir-tue, that is, the signs of its presence and the acts to which it leads. And since the signs of virtue, and such acts as it is the mark of a virtuous man to do or have done to him, are noble, it follows that all deeds or signs of courage, and everything done courageously, must be noble things; and so with what is just and actions done justly. (Not, however, actions justly done to us; here justice is unlike the other virtues; 'justly' does not always mean 'nobly'; when a man is punished, it is more shameful that this should be justly than unjustly done to him). The same is true of the other virtues. Again, those actions are noble for which the reward is simply honour, or

honour more than money. So are those in which a man aims
at something desirable for some one else's sake; actions good
absolutely, such as those a man does for his country without
thinking of himself; actions good in their own nature; actions
that are not good simply for the individual, since individual
interests are selfish. Noble also are those actions whose
advantage may be enjoyed after death, as opposed to those
whose advantage is enjoyed during one's lifetime: for the
latter are more likely to be for one's own sake only. Also, all
actions done for the sake of others, since these less than
other actions are done for one's own sake; and all successes
which benefit others and not oneself; and services done to
one's benefactors, for this is just; and good deeds generally,
since they are not directed to one's own profit. And the op-
posites of those things of which men feel ashamed, for men
are ashamed of saying, doing, or intending to do shameful
things. So when Alcaeus said

> Something I fain would say to thee,
> Only shame restraineth me,

Sappho wrote

> If for things good and noble thou wert yearning,
> If to speak baseness were thy tongue not burning,
> No load of shame would on thine eyelids weigh;
> What thou with honour wishest thou wouldst say.

Those things, also, are noble for which men strive anxiously,
without feeling fear; for they feel thus about the good things
which lead to fair fame. Again, one quality or action is
nobler than another if it is that of a naturally finer being:
thus a man's will be nobler than a woman's. And those
qualities are noble which give more pleasure to other people
than to their possessors; hence the nobleness of justice and
just actions. It is noble to avenge oneself on one's enemies

and not to come to terms with them; for requital is just, and the just is noble; and not to surrender is a sign of courage. Victory, too, and honour belong to the class of noble things, since they are desirable even when they yield no fruits, and they prove our superiority in good qualities. Things that deserve to be remembered are noble, and the more they deserve this, the nobler they are. So are the things that continue even after death; those which are always attended by honour; those which are exceptional; and those which are possessed by one person alone—these last are more readily remembered than others. So again are possessions that bring no profit, since they are more fitting than others for a gentleman. So are the distinctive qualities of a particular people, and the symbols of what it specially admires, like long hair in Sparta, where this is a mark of a free man, as it is not easy to perform any menial task when one's hair is long. Again, it is noble not to practise any sordid craft, since it is the mark of a free man not to live at another's beck and call. We are also to assume, when we wish either to praise a man or blame him, that qualities closely allied to those which he actually has are identical with them; for instance, that the cautious man is cold-blooded and treacherous, and that the stupid man is an honest fellow or the thick-skinned man a good-tempered one. We can always idealize any given man by drawing on the virtues akin to his actual qualities; thus we may say that the passionate and excitable man is 'outspoken'; or that the arrogant man is 'superb' or 'impressive'. Those who run to extremes will be said to possess the corresponding good qualities; rashness will be called courage, and extravagance generosity. That will be what most people think; and at the same time this method enables an advocate to draw a misleading inference from the motive, arguing that if a man runs into danger needlessly, much more will he do so in a noble cause; and if a man is open-handed to any one and every one, he will be so to his friends also, since it is the extreme form of goodness to be good to everybody. . . .

LUCIUS ANNAEUS SENECA

HOW MANY "CAUSES"?

YESTERDAY I shared with sickness; it claimed the forenoon and yielded the afternoon to me. First I tested my spirit with reading. Then when it passed this test I ventured upon larger demands, or rather gave it larger scope. I set to writing, and indeed with more than my customary concentration, for I was wrestling with a difficult subject where I refused to give in, until friends interceded and applied force to restrain me, like an invalid overdoing. Conversation supplanted composition. I now bring you the case under litigation; you have been designated arbiter. The assignment is more troublesome than you imagine, for the dispute is threefold.

As you know, we Stoics hold that there are two factors in nature which give rise to all things, cause and matter. Matter lies inert, susceptible to any use but yielding none if no one sets it in motion. Cause, which is to say reason, shapes matter and turns it where it will, to produce various objects. For any object raw material and a maker are requisite; one is matter, the other cause.

Every art is an imitation of nature. Apply the general principle I have stated to man's handiwork. A statue is the product of matter, which is susceptible to the artificer, and the artificer, who gives the matter its form. Here the material is bronze, the cause the craftsman. The same applies to everything; the material is one factor, the maker the other. The Stoics maintain that there is only one cause, the maker. Aristotle holds that "cause" has three connotations. "The first cause," he says, "is the matter itself, without which nothing can be produced. The second is the craftsman. The third is the form which is imposed on an individual product, as on a

1

statue." Form is what Aristotle calls *idos*. "There is, in addition, a fourth cause," Aristotle adds, "the purpose of the work as a whole." I shall explain. Bronze is the first cause of the statue, for it could never have been made if there were no material out of which it could be cast and modeled. The second cause is the craftsman, for the bronze could not have been given the statue's figure without expert hands to shape it. The third cause is form; the Doryphoros or Diadumenos would not have received their names unless their particular form had been imposed upon them. The fourth cause is the purpose of the work, for without one the statue would not have been made. What is this purpose? It is what motivated the artist, the object he pursued in making the statue. It might have been money, if he made it for sale, or glory, if he was bent on reputation, or religion, if he was preparing an offering for a temple. Purpose too, then, is a cause; or do you think a factor without which a thing could not have been produced is not to be reckoned among its causes?

To these Plato adds a fifth, the pattern, for which his name is "idea"; this is the thing the artist kept his eye on when he made the object he planned. It makes no difference whether he had an objective pattern to which he could actually turn his eyes or whether the pattern was within himself, a conception he himself had placed there. Such patterns of all things god has within himself; his mind encompasses the measures and numbers of absolutely everything which is to be acted upon. He is filled with the forms—eternal, unchanging, incorruptible—which Plato terms "ideas." Men may perish, therefore, but humanity, which is the pattern to which man is molded, persists, and though men suffer and die, the pattern is not subject to change. According to Plato, then, there are five causes: material, agent, form, pattern, purpose. Their product comes last. In the case of the statue, which was our point of departure, the material is the bronze, the agent the artist, the form is the figure given the material, the pattern the model the maker imitated, the purpose the object the maker had in view, and the product of all these the statue itself. The universe, as Plato asserts, possesses all these factors. The agent is god, the material matter, the form the contours and order of the visible universe, the pattern, of course, that according to which god created his mighty and magnificent work. Its purpose is his object in creating it. You ask what god's purpose may be? Goodness. So, at least, Plato says: "What was god's cause for creating the universe? He is good, and none that is good grudges anything good. His creation is therefore the best possible." Pronounce your sentence then, arbiter, and declare which formulation seems truest—not which *is* truest, for that is as far beyond us as truth itself.

The crowd of causes posited by Aristotle and Plato includes either too many or too few. If they regard as cause any factor whose absence would make the product impossible, they have named too few. They should reckon time among the causes, for nothing can be made without time. They should reckon place, for if there was no place for a thing to be made in, it could not be made. They should reckon motion, without which nothing comes into being or perishes. There is no art without motion, there is no change without motion. But the cause we are seeking is the primal and general cause. It must be simple, for matter too is simple. If we ask what this cause is, it is surely Creative Reason, which is to say, god. Those you listed are not a congeries of disparate causes but all depend on one, to wit, the creative cause. Do you hold that form is a cause? It is what the artist imposes upon his work, a part of the cause but not the cause. Neither is pattern a cause, but rather the cause's necessary instrument, as necessary to the artist as his chisel or rasp, without which his work cannot proceed. But these are neither parts of art nor causes of it. "The artist's purpose, what motivates him to create an object," it may be objected, "is its cause." Even if it is, it is not the efficient but an accessory cause, of which there are an infinite number; our investigation concerns the general cause. The position that the whole universe, which is a perfected work, is a cause, is not consistent with Aristotle's and Plato's customary acumen, for there is a wide difference between a work and the cause of the work.

Either pronounce sentence or take the easier course in such cases with a *non liquet* and an order to recapitulate. "Why," say you, "do you choose to waste time on questions which do not banish passions or master concupiscence?" It is a valid means for pacifying the mind that I deal with these problems and discuss them; first I scrutinize myself, and then the universe. Not even now am I wasting time, as you suppose. All these questions, provided they are not minced and fragmented into futile hair-splitting, uplift the soul and make it light when it is weighed down by a heavy load and eager to return whence it sprang. For body is a weight upon the soul and its punishment; under its pressure the soul is squeezed and trussed until philosophy comes to its support by prescribing contemplation of nature as a refreshment and directs it away from the earthy to the divine. This is the soul's liberation, this its enlargement; in the process it obtains release from the custody which constrains it and recovers its heavenly energy. Craftsmen engaged in fine work which strains and wearies the eyes go out into the open, if their light has been grudging and precarious, and refresh their vision with the free daylight in some spot devoted to the people's leisure; so the soul imprisoned in this dark and gloomy domicile seeks the open air as often as it can and finds refreshment in the contemplation of nature.

The wise man and the devotee of wisdom is indeed attached to his body, but in his better part he is elsewhere; his thoughts are directed to lofty matters. He is bound, as it were, by a military oath, and regards his life span as his term of enlistment. He is disciplined neither to love life nor hate it; he puts up with mortality, though he knows there is a fuller kind of existence. Will you forbid me examination of nature, will you distrain me from the whole and restrict me to a part? May I not inquire into the beginnings of all things, who shaped them, who sorted out matter that was heaped in an indiscriminate mass? May I not ask who the artificer of this universe is, what system reduced its huge bulk to law and order, or who gathered together what was scattered, sorted out what was confused, or distinguished the aspects of what lay inert in undifferentiated ugliness? What is the source of such outpouring of light? Is it fire or something brighter than fire? Should I not study such questions? Should I be ignorant of the region whence I descended? Am I to see all this once, or undergo repeated births? Where am I to go from here? What abode awaits my soul when it is released from the bondage of humanity? Do you forbid me to be concerned with heaven, which is to say, do you bid me live with head downcast? I am too big, I was born for a bigger destiny, than to be a chattel of my body, which in my own view is nothing else than a chain to fetter my freedom. My body I oppose to Fortune; upon it she may spend her force, but I will allow no wound to penetrate through it to myself. My body is the part of me that is subject to injury, my soul dwells in this vulnerable domicile. Never shall this flesh drive me to fear, never to assume a posture unworthy of a good man; never shall I lie out of consideration for this paltry body.

When it seems right I shall sever my partnership with it, and even now, while the attachment holds, we are not equal partners; the soul can claim complete jurisdiction. Contempt of body is unqualified freedom.

To come back to our subject, the contemplation of which I was just now speaking will contribute greatly to this freedom. All things consist of matter and god. God modulates matter, which is poured about him and follows him as guide and leader. The creative element, that is, god, is more powerful and more precious than matter, which is acted upon by god. The place god holds in the universe the soul holds in man. What is matter in the universe is body in us; the worse should therefore serve the better. We should be steadfast in the face of accident. We should not be apprehensive of injuries or wounds or chains or poverty. What is death? Either end or transition. I do not fear ceasing to be, for it is the same as not having begun to be; nor am I afraid of transition, for no alternative state can be so limiting. Farewell.

THE SOLE GOOD

YOU PROCLAIM a state of hostility if you are not kept informed of my doings day by day. See how frank I can be with you: I will even confide to you that I have been listening to a philosopher. This is the fifth day I have been attending; the lecture begins at two o'clock. "Very timely!" say you. But it *is* timely; what could be stupider than refusing to learn because you have not learned for a long time? "Do you mean that I must behave like a dandified undergraduate?" If this is the only thing that ill becomes my time of life I am well off. This school admits men of any age. "Do we get on in years to trail after youngsters?" If I go to the theater at my age and ride to the circus and insist on seeing every bout to its end, shall I blush to go to a philosopher?

A man should keep learning as long as he is ignorant, as the proverb has it, as long as he lives. And the principle applies most of all to my own study. As long as he lives a man should learn how to live. But there is something I teach in the school. What, you ask, do I teach? That even an old man should learn. When I step into the school I feel ashamed of the human race. To go to Metronax' house I must pass the theater of the Neapolitans, as you know. The place is packed. The point at issue is whether a man is a good flautist. The Greek piper and the herald also have their following. But in the place where the issue is "What is a good man?," and how a good man is to be defined, and how a man learns to be good, the audience is sparse, and even the few people there, the majority thinks, are not occupied in any business worth doing; they are called feckless and lazy. I would welcome such mockery. The reproaches of the ignorant should be received with mind imperturbable; a man making his way toward an ideal must be contemptuous of contempt.

Get on with it, Lucilius; hurry, don't let what happened to me happen to you; don't wait to be an elderly undergraduate. There is greater need to hurry because you have not touched the subject for a long while and it is one you can scarcely master when you are old. "How far can I advance?" As far as you try. What are you waiting for? Wisdom is never a windfall. Money may come unsought, office may be bestowed, influence and prestige may be thrust upon you, but virtue is not an accident. Even knowing virtue is no light or offhand task, but it is worth the effort to acquire all that is good at a stroke. For there is only one good, to wit, the honorable; the objectives commonly esteemed are neither true nor stable. I shall tell you why the honorable is the sole good for you, for you maintain that my earlier letter did not pursue the proposition far enough and consider that I applauded rather than demonstrated it.

I shall compress what has been said on the subject. Everything is valued by its particular good. Yield and bouquet commend the vine, fleetness the stag. The question in regard to a pack animal is the strength of his back, for his sole use is to carry freight. In a dog keenness is the primary consideration if he is to track game, fleetness if he is to overtake it, boldness if he is to come to close quarters and attack it. In every case the function for which a thing is created and by which it is rated ought to be the best. What is best in man? Reason, which puts him ahead of the animals and next to the gods. Perfect reason is, then, his peculiar good; his other qualities are common to animals and vegetables. He is strong; so are lions. He is handsome; so are peacocks. He is fleet; so are horses. My point is not that he is surpassed in all these qualities, for I am not asking what is greatest in him but what is peculiar to him. He has body; so have trees. He has impulses and can move at will; so can beasts and worms. He has a voice, but how much louder has a dog, shriller an eagle, deeper a bull, sweeter and of greater range a nightingale? What is peculiar to man? Reason. When this is right and perfected his measure of happiness is full. Hence, if an entity is praiseworthy and has attained the limit of its nature when it has perfected its peculiar good, and if man's peculiar good is reason, then if a man has perfected his reason he is praiseworthy and has attained the limit of his nature. This perfect reason is called virtue, and is equivalent to the honorable.

The sole good in man, therefore, is what is solely man's, for our question does not concern the good but the good of man. If nothing but reason is peculiarly man's, then reason is his sole good and balances all the rest. If a man is bad I presume he will be disapproved of, and if good, approved of. The gauge for approval or disapproval is his principal and unique quality. That this is a good there can be no doubt; you can doubt only whether it is the sole good. Now if a man possess all other qualities—health, wealth, long lineage, a crowded salon—but is confessedly bad, you will disapprove of him. Likewise, if a man possess none of the qualities I have listed but is without money, a throng of clients, nobility, a roster of grandparents and great-grandparents, but is confessedly good, you will approve of him. Consequently this is the one good of man, for the man who possesses it is praised though he lacks all else, and the man who lacks it is condemned and rejected despite his abundance of other qualities. What applies to man applies also to things. A ship is said to be good not when it is painted with costly colors or its beak coated with silver or gold or its mascot decorated with ivory reliefs, nor when it is loaded with state funds or regal treasure, but when it is stable and stanch and its seams tightly calked to keep the water out, and it is rugged enough to withstand the assaults of the sea, when it answers the rudder and is speedy and indifferent to the gale. You will call a sword good not when the baldric is gilt or the scabbard studded with gems but when its edge is sharp enough to slash and its point keen enough to pierce any protection. We do not ask how beautiful a rule is but how straight. Each thing is praised by reference to what is peculiar to it.

In man too, therefore, it is irrelevant to ask the extent of his plantations, the volume of his loans, the number of his clients, the costliness of the bed he lies on, or the transparency of the cups he drinks out of; the point is, how good is he? He is good if his reason is straightforward and upright and suited to the will of his nature. This is called virtue, this is the honorable, and man's unique good. For whereas reason perfects man, perfect reason makes him blessed; what makes a man blessed is his sole good. We maintain that what proceeds out of virtue and is involved in it, that is to say, all its works, are also good; but virtue itself is the sole good because there is no good without it. If every good is in the soul, then whatever stabilizes, raises, and enlarges the soul is good; but virtue does make the soul stronger, loftier, and more spacious. Other things which prick our concupiscence depress the soul and unhinge it, and while they appear to uplift it they are in fact inflating it and beguiling it with utter vanity. The only good, therefore, is what makes the soul better.

Every action of the whole of life is regulated by consideration of the honorable and the base. The rationale for acting or not acting is controlled by this consideration. I will tell you how this is. A good man will do what he thinks will be honorable for him to do even if it is laborious, he will do it even if it is damaging to him, he will do it even if it is dangerous. On the other hand, he will not do what is base even if it brings him money, even if it brings him pleasure, even if it brings him power. Nothing can deflect him from what is honorable, nothing tempt him to what is base. Hence, if he is bound to pursue the honorable course at all costs and to eschew the base at all costs and to look to these two principles in every act of his life, equating the good with the honorable and the bad with the base, if his virtue is wholly uncorrupted and maintains its bearings, then virtue is his sole good and it is impossible for any accident to make it otherwise. He has escaped the danger of change; folly may creep toward wisdom, but wisdom does not backslide to folly.

I have said, as you may recall, that irrational impulse has driven many a man to trample over things commonly cherished or dreaded. There are cases where a man has thrust his arm into the flames, has laughed in the face of his torturers, has shed no tear at the death of his children, has gone unfalteringly to his death. Love or anger or lust have thrown the gauntlet down. What a spurt of obstinacy flaring up under some stimulus can achieve, surely virtue, whose power is not impulsive or sudden but consistent and whose strength is enduring, can do. It follows that what the irrational can scorn occasionally and the wise regularly is neither good nor evil. The sole good is therefore virtue itself, which strides between this lot and that and despises both equally.

If you entertain the view that there is any good beside the honorable, then every virtue will be hamstrung. None can be maintained if it must look to something outside itself. If there is any such thing it must conflict with reason, from which the virtues derive, and with truth, which is impossible without reason. And any opinion in conflict with truth is false. A good man, you cannot but agree, has full piety toward the gods. Whatever happens to him he will bear with serenity because he knows it has happened by the divine law which governs the universe. That being the case, he will have one sole good, to wit, the honorable; this involves obedience to the gods, not flaring up at sudden contretemps or deploring one's lot, but accepting fate patiently and fulfilling its commands. If there is a good other than the honorable, we shall be hounded by greed for life and greed for life's comforts. This is boundless, undefined, and intolerable; the honorable is definable, and hence the sole good.

I have remarked that human life would be happier than the gods' if the things that the gods do not use, such as money and magistracies, were goods. Furthermore, if souls released from the body do indeed survive, the state that awaits them is happier than while they are involved with body. And if things of which we make bodily use are goods, then our souls will be worse off when they are released; but it is incredible that souls imprisoned and besieged are happier than souls liberated and given freedom of the universe. I also remarked that if what man has in common with dumb animals are goods, then animals could lead a happy life; but this is altogether impossible. For the sake of the honorable we must put up with anything, which we need not do if there were any good other than the honorable. I have dealt with these arguments more fully in an earlier letter; here I have compressed them and run through them summarily.

Such a view as this will never strike you as true unless you raise your soul and ask yourself whether, if an exigency demanded that you die for your country and ransom the safety of your fellow citizens by your own, you would put your neck out not only patiently but gladly. If you would do such a thing then there is no other good, for you relinquish all else to possess this alone. See what force the honorable has! You will die for your country when you know you ought, even if you must do so forthwith. Sometimes noble action wins great joy, momentary and brief though it be, and though no profit of his achievement will accrue to a man who has run his course and is released from human concerns, yet the very contemplation of what is to be is a delight; when the brave and righteous man contemplates what his death will buy, his country's liberty and the salvation of those for whom he is laying his life down, he attains the height of pleasure and rejoices in his own jeopardy. But even the man who is deprived of the joy which fingering his greatest and last achievement affords will leap to his death without hesitation, content that his action is right and dutiful. Confront him even now with many deterrents; say to him, "Your deed will speedily be forgotten, public opinion is ingrate," and he will answer, "Those things are extraneous to my job, which is all I have to think of. I know that it is honorable, and so I go wherever it leads and calls me."

This then is the only good, and it is perceived not only by the perfect soul but by the generous and well-endowed also; other goods are frivolous and transitory. That is why possession of them is attended by anxiety. Even if by Fortune's favor they are piled in a heap, they are a heavy incubus upon their owners; always they press down upon them and sometimes they crush them. None of that purple-clad group is happy, any more than the players whose roles bestow scepter and cape upon them; before their audience they strut buskined and expansive, but at the stage door they are unshod and return to their own figure. None raised to a higher pinnacle by riches or magistracies is great. Why then does he seem to be? Because you include his pedestal in the measurement. A dwarf is not big even if he stands on a mountain top, and a colossus retains his stature even if he stands in a well. This is the mistake which misleads us; we are imposed upon because we never estimate a man by what he is but add his trappings on. If you wish to arrive at a true estimate of a man and understand his quality, look at him naked. Make him lay aside his inheritance, his titles, Fortune's other specious trimmings; make him lay even his body aside and look at his soul to ascertain its quality and size and whether its greatness is its own or detachable.

If a man can look at flashing swords with eyes unswerving, if he knows that it is of no moment to him whether his soul departs through mouth or throat, call him happy. Call him happy if, when physical torture is decreed for him, whether by some accident or by *force majeure,* if with mind unperturbed he hears of chains and exile and the empty terrors of mankind and says (*Aeneid* 6.103 ff.):

> "No new fashion of hardship, none unexpected
> Rises to confront me; all have I anticipated,
> All have I traversed in my mind—

Today it is you that confront me with this doom; I have always confronted myself with it, and as a man am prepared for a man's lot." The blow of an anticipated evil falls soft. Fools, however, and those who trust Fortune find every "fashion new and unexpected." For the untaught a large portion of the evil is its novelty. The proof is that men bear with fortitude, when they have grown accustomed to them, things they had thought very difficult. The sage accustoms himself to evils before they come, and what others make easy by long toleration he makes easy by long cogitation. Sometimes we hear the untaught say, "I knew this was in store for me"; the sage knows that everything is in store for him, and whatever happens he says, "I knew it." Farewell.

PLUTARCH was born about A.D. 46 in Boeotia. He studied philosophy in Athens. Afterward he lived for a period in Rome, where he lectured on philosophy and undertook the education of Hadrian. The Emperor Trajan bestowed consular rank upon him, and Hadrian, when he succeeded to the throne, appointed Plutarch procurator of Greece. Eventually he returned to his native town, where he became a priest in the temple of Delphi. Plutarch's great work, the *Lives,* is thought to have been written in his later years. The *Lives* consists of forty-six biographies arranged in pairs, one Greek life and one comparable Roman life, except for four single biographies. The Roman Marcus Cato is paired with the Greek Aristides. Among the great figures of antiquity whom Plutarch included in the *Lives* are Solon, Pericles, Pompey, Alexander, Caesar, and Cicero. The *Lives* provide the factual basis for four of Shakespeare's plays and have been a very important influence in English literature generally. A lesser known work by Plutarch, the *Moralia,* consists of dialogues and essays on ethical, literary, and historical subjects. Apart from their own literary value, Plutarch's works contain in many cases the only record we have of certain lost works of antiquity. He died in the city of his birth about A.D. 120.

PLUTARCH

Lives
MARCUS CATO

NUMBER **3**

SET FIVE

THE GREAT BOOKS FOUNDATION *Chicago*

*The special contents of this edition are copyright 1963
by* THE GREAT BOOKS FOUNDATION. *This selection has been specially
edited for the Junior Great Books discussion program.*

Printed in the United States of America.

published and distributed by

THE GREAT BOOKS FOUNDATION
a non-profit corporation
5 South Wabash Avenue, Chicago 3, Illinois

LIVES

MARCUS CATO

MARCUS CATO, we are told, was born at Tusculum, though (till he betook himself to civil and military affairs) he lived and was bred up in the country of the Sabines, where his father's estate lay. His ancestors seeming almost entirely unknown, he himself praises his father Marcus, as a worthy man and a brave soldier, and Cato, his great-grandfather, too, as one who had often obtained military prizes, and who, having lost five horses under him, received, on the account of his valour, the worth of them out of the public exchequer. Now it being the custom among the Romans to call those who, having no repute by birth, made themselves eminent by their own exertions, new men or upstarts, they called even Cato himself so, and so he confessed himself to be as to any public distinction or employment, but yet asserted that in the exploits and virtues of his ancestors he was very ancient. His third name originally was not Cato, but Priscus, though afterwards he had the surname of Cato, by reason of his abilities; for the Romans call a skilful or experienced man *Catus*. He was of a ruddy complexion and grey-eyed; as the writer, who, with no good-will, made the following epigram upon him lets us see:—

> "Porcius, who snarls at all in every place,
> With his grey eyes, and with his fiery face,
> Even after death will scarce admitted be
> Into the infernal realms by Hecate."

He gained, in early life, a good habit of body by working with his own hands, and living temperately, and serving in war; and seemed to have an equal proportion both of health and strength. And he exerted and practised his eloquence through all the neighbourhood and little villages; thinking it as requisite as a second body, and an all but necessary organ to one who looks forward to something above a mere humble and inactive life. He would never refuse to be counsel for those who needed him, and was, indeed, early reckoned a good lawyer, and, ere long, a capable orator.

Hence his solidity and depth of character showed itself gradually more and more to those with whom he was concerned, and claimed, as it were, employment in great affairs and places of public command. Nor did he merely abstain from taking fees for his counsel and pleading, but did not even seem to put any high price on the honour which proceeded from such kind of combats, seeming much more desirous to signalise himself in the camp and in real fights; and while yet but a youth, had his breast covered with scars he had received from the enemy: being (as he himself says) but seventeen years old when he made his first campaign; in the time when Hannibal, in the height of his success, was burning and pillaging all Italy. In engagements he would strike boldly, without flinching, stand firm to his ground, fix a bold countenance upon his enemies, and with a harsh threatening voice accost them, justly thinking himself and telling others that such a rugged kind of behaviour sometimes terrifies the enemy more than the sword itself. In his marches he bore his own arms on foot, whilst one servant only followed, to carry the provision for his table, with whom he is said never to have been angry or hasty whilst he made ready his dinner or supper, but would, for the most part, when he was free from military duty, assist and help himself to dress it. When he was with the army, he used to drink only water; unless, perhaps, when extremely thirsty, he might mingle it with a little vinegar, or if he found his strength fail him, take a little wine.

The little country house of Manius Curius, who had been thrice carried in triumph, happened to be near his farm; so that often going thither, and contemplating the small compass of the place, and plainness of the dwelling, he formed an idea of the mind of the person, who being one of the greatest of the Romans, and having subdued the most warlike nations, nay, had driven Pyrrhus out of Italy now, after three triumphs, was contented to dig in so small a piece of ground, and live in such a cottage. Here it was that the ambassadors of the Samnites, finding him boiling turnips in the chimney corner, offered him a present of gold; but he sent them away with this saying; that he, who was content with such a supper, had no need of gold; and that he thought it more honourable to conquer those who possessed the gold, than to possess the gold itself. Cato, after reflecting upon these things, used to return and, reviewing his own farm, his servants, and housekeeping, increase his labour and retrench all superfluous expenses.

When Fabius Maximus took Tarentum, Cato, being then but a youth, was a soldier under him; and being lodged with one Nearchus, a Pythagorean, desired to understand some of his doctrine, and hearing from him the language, which Plato also uses—that pleasure is evil's chief bait; the body the principal calamity of the soul; and that those thoughts which most separate and take it off from the affections of the body most enfranchise and purify it; he fell in love the more with frugality and temperance. With this exception, he is said not to have studied Greek until when he was pretty old; and in rhetoric to have then profited a little by Thucydides, but more by Demosthenes; his writings, however, are considerably embellished with Greek sayings and stories; nay, many of these, translated word for word, are placed with his own apothegms and sentences.

There was a man of the highest rank, and very influential among the Romans, called Valerius Flaccus, who was singularly skilful in discerning excellence yet in the bud, and also much disposed to nourish and advance it. He, it seems, had lands bordering upon Cato's; nor could he but admire when he understood from his servants the manner of his living, how he laboured with his own hands, went on foot betimes in the morning to the courts to assist those who wanted his counsel: how, returning home again, when it was winter, he would throw a loose frock over his shoulders, and in the summer time would work without anything on among his domestics, sit down with them, eat of the same bread, and drink of the same wine. When they spoke, also, of other good qualities, his fair dealing and moderation, mentioning also some of his wise sayings, he ordered that he should be invited to supper; and thus becoming personally assured of his fine temper and his superior character, which, like a plant, seemed only to require culture and a better situation, he urged and persuaded him to apply himself to state affairs at Rome. Thither, therefore, he went, and by his pleading soon gained many friends and admirers; but, Valerius chiefly assisting his promotion, he first of all got appointed tribune in the army, and afterwards was made quaestor, or treasurer. And now becoming eminent and noted, he passed, with Valerius himself, through the greatest commands, being first his colleague as consul, and then censor. But among all the ancient senators, he most attached himself to Fabius Maximus; not so much for the honour of his person, and the greatness of his power, as that he might have before him his habit and manner of life, as the best examples to follow; and so he did not hesitate to oppose Scipio the Great, who, being then but a young man, seemed to set himself against the power of Fabius, and to be envied by him. For being sent together with him as treasurer, when he saw him, according to his natural custom, make great expenses, and distribute among the soldiers without sparing, he freely told him that the expense in itself was not the greatest thing to be considered, but that he was corrupting the frugality of the soldiers, by giving them the means to abandon themselves to unnecessary pleasures and luxuries. Scipio answered, that he had no need for so accurate a treasurer (bearing on as he was, so to say, full sail to the war), and that he owed the people an account of his actions, and not of the money he spent. Hereupon Cato returned from Sicily and, together with Fabius, made loud complaints in the open senate of Scipio's lavishing unspeakable sums, and childishly loitering away his time in wrestling matches and comedies, as if he were not to make war, but holiday; and thus succeeded in getting some of the tribunes of the people sent to call him back to Rome, in case the accusations should prove true. But Scipio demonstrating, as it were, to them, by his preparations, the coming victory, and, being found merely to be living pleasantly with his friends, when there was nothing else to do, but in no respect because of that easiness and liberality at all the more negligent in things of consequence and moment, without impediment, set sail toward the war.

Cato grew more and more powerful by his eloquence, so that he was commonly called the Roman Demosthenes; but his manner of life was yet more famous and talked of. For oratorical skill was, as an accomplishment, commonly studied and sought after by all young men; but he was very rare who would cultivate the old habits of bodily labour, or prefer a light supper, and a breakfast which never saw the fire, or be in love with poor clothes and a homely lodging, or could set his ambition rather on doing without luxuries than on possessing them. For now the state, unable to keep its purity by reason of its greatness, and having so many affairs, and people from all parts under its government, was fain to admit many mixed customs and new examples of living. With reason, therefore, everybody admired Cato, when they saw others sink under labours and grow effeminate by pleasures; and yet beheld him unconquered by either, and that not only when he was young and desirous of honour, but also when old and grey-headed, after a consulship and triumph; like some famous victor in the games, persevering in his exercise and maintaining his character to the very last. He himself says that he never wore a suit of clothes which cost more than a hundred drachmas; and that, when he was general and consul, he drank the same wine which his workmen did; and that the meat or fish which was bought in the meat-market for his dinner did not cost above thirty *asses*. All which was for the sake of the commonwealth, that so his body might be the hardier for the war. Having a piece of embroidered Babylonian tapestry left him, he sold it; because none of his farmhouses were so much as plastered. Nor did he ever buy a slave for above fifteen hundred drachmas; as he did not seek for . . . handsome ones, but able sturdy workmen, horse-keepers and cow-herds: and these he thought ought to be sold again, when they grew old, and no useless servants fed in the house. In short, he reckoned nothing a good bargain which was superfluous; but whatever it was, though sold for a farthing, he would think it a great price, if you had no need of it; and was for the purchase of lands for sowing and feeding, rather than grounds for sweeping and watering.

Some imputed these things to petty avarice, but others approved of him, as if he had only the more strictly denied himself for the rectifying and amending of others. Yet certainly, in my judgment, it marks an over-rigid temper for a man to take the work out of his servants as out of brute beasts, turning them off and selling them in their old age, and thinking there ought to be no further commerce between man and man than whilst there arises some profit by it. We see that kindness or humanity has a larger field than bare justice to exercise itself in; law and justice we cannot, in the nature of things, employ on others than men; but we may extend our goodness and charity even to irrational creatures; and such acts flow from a gentle nature, as water from an abundant spring. It is doubtless the part of a kind-natured man to keep even worn-out horses and dogs, and not only take care of them when they are foals and whelps, but also when they are grown old. The Athenians, when they built their Hecatompedon, turned those mules loose to feed freely which they had observed to have done the hardest labour. One of these (they say) came once of itself to offer its service, and ran along with, nay, and went before, the teams which drew the waggons up to the acropolis, as if it would incite and encourage them to draw more stoutly; upon which there passed a vote that the creature should be kept at the public charge even till it died. The graves of Cimon's horses, which thrice won the Olympian races, are yet to be seen close by his own monument. Old Xanthippus, too (amongst many others who buried the dogs they had bred up), entombed his which swam after his galley to Salamis, when the people fled from Athens, on the top of a cliff, which they call the Dog's Tomb to this day. Nor are we to use living creatures like old shoes or dishes and throw them away when they are worn out or broken with service; but if it were for nothing else, but by way of study and practice in humanity, a man ought always to prehabituate himself in these things to be of a kind and sweet disposition. As to myself, I would not so much as sell my draught ox on the account of his age, much less for a small piece of money sell a poor old man, and so chase him, as it were, from his own country, by turning him not only out of the place where he has lived a long while, but also out of the manner of living he has been accustomed to, and that more especially when he would be as useless to the buyer as to the seller. Yet Cato for all this glories that he left that very horse in Spain which he used in the wars when he was consul, only because he would not put the public to the charge of his freight. Whether these acts are to be ascribed to the greatness or pettiness of his spirit, let every one argue as they please.

For his general temperance, however, and self-control he really deserves the highest admiration. For when he commanded the army, he never took for himself, and those that belonged to him, above three bushels of wheat for a month, and somewhat less than a bushel and a half a day of barley for his baggage-cattle. And when he entered upon the government of Sardinia, where his predecessors had been used to require tents, bedding and clothes upon the public account, and to charge the state heavily with the cost of provisions and entertainments for a great train of servants and friends, the difference he showed in his economy was something incredible. There was nothing of any sort for which he put the public to expense; he would walk without a carriage to visit the cities, with one only of the common town officers, who carried his dress, and a cup to offer libation with. Yet though he seemed thus easy and sparing to all who were under his power, he, on the other hand, showed most inflexible severity and strictness in what related to public justice, and was rigorous and precise in what concerned the ordinances of the commonwealth; so that the Roman government never seemed more terrible, nor yet more mild than under his administration.

His very manner of speaking seemed to have such a kind of idea with it; for it was courteous, and yet forcible; pleasant, yet overwhelming; facetious, yet austere; sententious, and yet vehement; like Socrates, in the description of Plato, who seemed outwardly to those about him to be but a simple, talkative, blunt fellow; whilst at the bottom he was full of such gravity and matter, as would even move tears and touch the very hearts of his auditors. And, therefore, I know not what has persuaded some to say that Cato's style was chiefly like that of Lysias. However, let us leave those to judge of these things who profess most to distinguish between the several kinds of oratorical style in Latin; whilst we write down some of his memorable sayings; being of the opinion that a man's character appears much more by his words than, as some think it does, by his looks.

Being once desirous to dissuade the common people of Rome from their unseasonable and impetuous clamour for largesses and distributions of corn, he began thus to harangue them: "It is a difficult task, O citizens, to make speeches to the belly, which has no ears." Reproving, also, their sumptuous habits, he said it was hard to preserve a city where a fish sold for more than an ox. He had a saying, also, that the Roman people were like sheep; for they, when single, do not obey, but when altogether in a flock, they follow their leaders: "So you," said he, "when you have got together in a body, let yourselves be guided by those whom singly you would never think of being advised by." Discoursing of the power of women: "Men," said he, "usually command women; but we command all men, and the women command us." But this, indeed, is borrowed from the sayings of Themistocles, who, when his son was making many demands of him by means of the mother, said, "O woman, the Athenians govern the Greeks; I govern the Athenians, but you govern me, and your son governs you; so let him use his power sparingly since, simple as he is, he can do more than all the Greeks together." Another saying of Cato's was, that the Roman people did not only fix the value of such and such purple dyes, but also of such and such habits of life: "For," said he, "as dyers most of all dye such colours as they see to be most agreeable, so the young men learn, and zealously affect, what is most popular with you." He also exhorted them that, if they were grown great by their virtue and temperance, they should not change for the worse; but if intemperance and vice had made them great, they should change for the better; for by that means they were grown indeed quite great enough. He would say, likewise, of men who wanted to be continually in office, that apparently they did not know their road; since they could not do without beadles to guide them on it. He also reproved the citizens for choosing still the same men as their magistrates: "For you will seem," said he, "either not to esteem government worth much, or to think few worthy to hold it." Speaking, too, of a certain enemy of his, who lived a very base and discreditable life: "It is considered," he said, "rather as a curse than a blessing on him, that this fellow's mother prays that she may leave him behind her." Pointing at one who had sold the land which his father had left him, and which lay near the seaside, he pretended to express his wonder at his being stronger even than the sea itself; for what it washed away with a great deal of labour, he with a great deal of ease drank away. When the senate, with a great deal of splendour, received King Eumenes on his visit to Rome, and the chief citizens strove who should be most about him, Cato appeared to regard him with suspicion and apprehension; and when one that stood by, too, took occasion to say that he was a very good prince and a great lover of the Romans: "It may be so," said Cato; "but by nature this same animal of a king is a kind of man-eater"; nor, indeed, were there ever kings who deserved to be compared with Epaminondas, Pericles, Themistocles, Manius Curius, or Hamilcar, surnamed Barcas. He used to say, too, that his enemies envied him because he had to get up every day before light and neglect his own business to follow that of the public. He would also tell you that he had rather be deprived of the reward for doing well than not to suffer the punishment for doing ill; and that he could pardon all offenders but himself.

The Romans having sent three ambassadors to Bithynia, of whom one was gouty, another had his skull trepanned, and the other seemed little better than a fool, Cato, laughing, gave out that the Romans had sent an embassy which had neither feet, head, nor heart. His interest being entreated by Scipio, on account of Polybius, for the Achaean exiles, and there happening to be a great discussion in the senate about it, some being for, and some against their return, Cato, standing up, thus delivered himself: "Here do we sit all day long, as if we had nothing to do but beat our brains whether these old Greeks should be carried to their graves by the bearers here or by those in Achaea." The senate voting their return, it seems that a few days after Polybius's friends further wished that it should be further moved in the senate that the said banished persons should receive again the honours which they first had in Achaea; and to this purpose they sounded Cato for his opinion; but he, smiling, answered, that Polybius, Ulysses like, having escaped out of the Cyclops' den, wanted, it would seem, to go back again because he had left his cap and belt behind him. He used to assert, also, that wise men profited more by fools, than fools by wise men; for that wise men avoided the faults of fools, but that fools would not imitate the good examples of wise men. He would profess, too, that he was more taken with young men that blushed than with those who looked pale; and that he never desired to have a soldier that moved his hands too much in marching, and his feet too much in fighting; or snored louder than he shouted. Ridiculing a fat, overgrown man: "What use," said he, "can the state turn a man's body to, when all between the throat and groin is taken up by the belly?" When one who was much given to pleasures desired his acquaintance, begging his pardon, he said he could not live with a man whose palate was of a quicker sense than his heart. He would likewise say that the soul of a lover lived in the body of another: and that in his whole life he most repented of three things; one was, that he had trusted a secret to a woman; another, that he went by water when he might have gone by land; the third, that he had remained one whole day without doing any business of moment. Applying himself to an old man who was committing some vice: "Friend," said he, "old age has of itself blemishes enough; do not you add to it the deformity of vice." Speaking to a tribune, who was reputed a poisoner, and was very violent for the bringing in of a bill, in order to make a certain law: "Young man," cried he, "I know not which would be better, to drink, what you mix, or confirm what you would put up for a law." Being reviled by a fellow who lived a profligate and wicked life: "A contest," replied he, "is unequal between you and me: for you can hear ill words easily, and can as easily give them: but it is unpleasant to me to give such, and unusual to hear them." Such was his manner of expressing himself in his memorable sayings.

Being chosen consul, with his friend and familiar Valerius Flaccus, the government of that part of Spain which the Romans called the Hither Spain fell to his lot. Here, as he was engaged in reducing some of the tribes by force, and bringing over others by good words, a large army of barbarians fell upon him, so that there was danger of being disgracefully forced out again. He therefore called upon his neighbours, the Celtiberians, for help; and on their demanding two hundred talents for their assistance, everybody else thought it intolerable that even the Romans should promise barbarians a reward for their aid; but Cato said there was no discredit or harm in it; for, if they overcame, they would pay them out of the enemy's purse, and not out of their own; but if they were overcome, there would be nobody left either to demand the reward or to pay it. However, he won that battle completely, and, after that, all his other affairs succeeded splendidly. Polybius says that, by his command, the walls of all the cities on this side the river Baetis were in one day's time demolished, and yet there were a great many of them full of brave and warlike men. Cato himself says that he took more cities than he stayed days in Spain. Neither is this a mere rhodomontade, if it be true that the number was four hundred. And though the soldiers themselves had got much in the fights, yet he distributed a pound of silver to every man of them, saying, it was better that many of the Romans should return home with silver, rather than a few with gold. For himself, he affirms, that of all the things that were taken, nothing came to him beyond what he ate and drank. "Neither do I find fault," continued he, "with those that seek to profit by these spoils, but I had rather compete in valour with the best, than in wealth with the richest, or with the most covetous in love of money." Nor did he merely keep himself clear from taking anything, but even all those who more immediately belonged to him. He had five servants with him in the army; one of whom called Paccus, bought three boys out of those who were taken captive; which Cato coming to understand, the man, rather than venture into his presence, hanged himself. Cato sold the boys, and carried the price he got for them into the public exchequer.

Scipio the Great, being his enemy, and desiring, whilst he was carrying all things so successfully, to obstruct him, and take the affairs of Spain into his own hands, succeeded in getting himself appointed his successor in the government, and, making all possible haste, put a term to Cato's authority. But he, taking with him a convoy of five cohorts of foot and five hundred horse to attend him home, overthrew by the way the Lacetanians, and taking from them six hundred deserters, caused them all to be beheaded; upon which Scipio seemed to be in indignation, but Cato, in mock disparagement of himself, said, "Rome would become great indeed, if the most honourable and great men would not yield up the first place of valour to those who were more obscure, and when they who were of the commonalty (as he himself was) would contend in valour with those who were most eminent in birth and honour." The senate having voted to change nothing of what had been established by Cato, the government passed away under Scipio to no manner of purpose, in idleness and doing nothing; and so diminished his credit much more than Cato's. Nor did Cato, who now received a triumph, remit after this and slacken the reins of virtue, as many do, who strive not so much for virtue's sake, as for vainglory, and having attained the highest honours, as the consulship and triumphs, pass the rest of their life in pleasure and idleness, and quit all public affairs. But he, like those who are just entered upon public life for the first time, and thirst after gaining honour and glory in some new office, strained himself, as if he were but just setting out; and offering still publicly his service to his friends and citizens, would give up neither his pleadings nor his soldiery.

He accompanied and assisted Tiberius Sempronius, as his lieutenant, when he went into Thrace and to the Danube; and, in the quality of tribune, went with Manius Acilius into Greece, against Antiochus the Great, who, after Hannibal, more than any one struck terror into the Romans. For having reduced once more under a single command almost the whole of Asia, all, namely, that Seleucus Nicator had possessed, and having brought into obedience many warlike nations of the barbarians, he longed to fall upon the Greeks, as if they only were now worthy to fight with him. So across he came with his forces, pretending, as a specious cause of the war, that it was to free the Greeks, who had indeed no need of it, they having been but newly delivered from the power of king Philip and the Macedonians, and made independent, with the free use of their own laws, by the goodness of the Romans themselves: so that all Greece was in commotion and excitement, having been corrupted by the hopes of royal aid which the popular leaders in their cities put them into. Manius, therefore, sent ambassadors to the different cities; and Titus Flaminius (as is written in the account of him) suppressed and quieted most of the attempts of the innovators, without any trouble. Cato brought over the Corinthians, those of Patrea and Aegium, and spent a good deal of time at Athens. There is also an oration of his said to be extant which he spoke in Greek to the people; in which he expressed his admiration of the virtue of the ancient Athenians, and signified that he came with a great deal of pleasure to be a spectator of the beauty and greatness of their city. But this is a fiction; for he spoke to the Athenians by an interpreter, though he was able to have spoken himself; but he wished to observe the usage of his own country, and laughed at those who admired nothing but what was in Greek. Jesting upon Postumius Albinus, who had written an historical work in Greek, and requested that allowances might be made for his attempt, he said that allowance indeed might be made if he had done it under the express compulsion of an Amphictyonic decree. The Athenians, he says, admired the quickness and vehemence of his speech; for an interpreter would be very long in repeating what he expressed with a great deal of brevity; but on the whole he professed to believe that the words of the Greeks came only from their lips, whilst those of the Romans came from their hearts.

Now Antiochus, having occupied with his army the narrow passages about Thermopylae, and added palisades and walls to the natural fortifications of the place, sat down there, thinking he had done enough to divert the war; and the Romans, indeed, seemed wholly to despair of forcing the passage; but Cato, calling to mind the compass and circuit which the Persians had formerly made to come at this place, went forth in the night, taking along with him part of the army. Whilst they were climbing up, the guide, who was a prisoner, missed the way, and wandering up and down by impracticable and precipitous paths, filled the soldiers with fear and despondency. Cato, perceiving the danger, commanded all the rest to halt, and stay where they were, whilst he himself, taking along with him one Lucius Manlius, a most expert man at climbing mountains, went forward with a great deal of labour and danger, in the dark night, and without the least moonshine, among the wild olive-trees and steep craggy rocks, there being nothing but precipices and darkness before their eyes, till they struck into a little pass which they thought might lead down into the enemy's camp. There they put up marks upon some conspicuous peaks which surmount the hill called Callidromon, and, returning again, they led the army along with them to the said marks, till they got into their little path again, and there once made a halt; but when they began to go further, the path deserted them at a precipice, where they were in another strait and fear; nor did they perceive that they were all this while near the enemy. And now the day began to give some light, when they seemed to hear a noise, and presently after to see the Greek trenches and the guard at the foot of the rock. Here, therefore, Cato halted his forces, and commanded the troops from Firmum only, without the rest, to stick by him, as he had always found them faithful and ready. And when they came up and formed around him in close order, he thus spoke to them: "I desire," he said, "to take one of the enemy alive, that so I may understand what men these are who guard the passage; their number; and with what discipline, order, and preparation they expect us; but this feat," continued he, "must be an act of a great deal of quickness and boldness, such as that of lions, when they dart upon some timorous animal." Cato had no sooner thus expressed himself, but the Firmans forthwith rushed down the mountain, just as they were, upon the guard, and, falling unexpectedly upon them, affrighted and dispersed them all. One armed man they took, and brought to Cato, who quickly learned from him that the rest of the forces lay in the narrow passage about the king; that those who kept the tops of the rocks were six hundred choice Aetolians. Cato, therefore, despising the smallness of their number and carelessness, forthwith drawing his sword, fell upon them with a great noise of trumpets and shouting. The enemy, perceiving them thus tumbling, as it were, upon them from the precipices, flew to the main body, and put all things into disorder there.

In the meantime, whilst Manius was forcing the works below, and pouring the thickest of his forces into the narrow passages, Antiochus was hit in the mouth with a stone, so that his teeth being beaten out by it, he felt such excessive pain, that he was fain to turn away with his horse; nor did any part of his army stand the shock of the Romans. Yet, though there seemed no reasonable hope of flight, where all paths were so difficult, and where there were deep marshes and steep rocks, which looked as if they were ready to receive those who should stumble, the fugitives, nevertheless, crowding and pressing together in the narrow passages, destroyed even one another in their terror of the swords and blows of the enemy. Cato (as it plainly appears) was never oversparing of his own praises, and seldom shunned boasting of any exploit; which quality, indeed, he seems to have thought the natural accompaniment of great actions; and with these particular exploits he was highly puffed up; he says that those who saw him that day pursuing and slaying the enemies were ready to assert that Cato owed not so much to the public as the public did to Cato; nay, he adds, that Manius the consul, coming hot from the fight, embraced him for a great while, when both were all in a sweat; and then cried out with joy that neither he himself, no, nor all the people together, could make him a recompense equal to his actions. After the fight he was sent to Rome, that he himself might be the messenger of it: and so, with a favourable wind, he sailed to Brundusium, and in one day got from thence to Tarentum; and having travelled four days more, upon the fifth, counting from the time of his landing, he arrived at Rome, and so brought the first news of the victory himself; and filled the whole city with joy and sacrifices, and the people with the belief that they were able to conquer every sea and every land.

These are pretty nearly all the eminent actions of Cato relating to military affairs: in civil policy, he was of opinion that one chief duty consisted in accusing and indicting criminals. He himself prosecuted many, and he would also assist others who prosecuted them, nay, would even procure such, as he did the Petilii against Scipio; but not being able to destroy him, by reason of the nobleness of his family, and the real greatness of his mind, which enabled him to trample all calumnies under foot, Cato at last would meddle no more with him; yet joining with the accusers against Scipio's brother Lucius, he succeeded in obtaining a sentence against him, which condemned him to the payment of a large sum of money to the state; and being insolvent, and in danger of being thrown into jail, he was, by the interposition of the tribunes of the people, with much ado dismissed. It is also said of Cato, that when he met a certain youth, who had effected the disgrace of one of his father's enemies, walking in the market-place, he shook him by the hand, telling him, that this was what we ought to sacrifice to our dead parents —not lambs and goats, but the tears and condemnations of their adversaries. But neither did he himself escape with impunity in his management of affairs; for if he gave his enemies but the least hold, he was still in danger, and exposed to be brought to justice. He is reported to have escaped at least fifty indictments; and one above the rest, which was the last, when he was eighty-six years old, about which time he uttered the well-known saying, that it was hard for him who had lived with one generation of men, to plead now before another. Neither did he make this the least of his lawsuits; for, four years after, when he was fourscore and ten, he accused Servilius Galba: so that his life and actions extended, we may say, as Nestor's did, over three ordinary ages of man. For, having had many contests, as we have related, with Scipio the Great, about affairs of state, he continued them down to Scipio the younger, who was the adopted grandson of the former, and the son of that Paulus who overthrew Perseus and the Macedonians.

Ten years after his consulship, Cato stood for the office of censor, which was indeed the summit of all honour, and in a manner the highest step in civil affairs; for besides all other power, it had also that of an inquisition into every one's life and manners. For the Romans thought that no marriage, or rearing of children, nay, no feast or drinking-bout, ought to be permitted according to every one's appetite or fancy, without being examined and inquired into; being indeed of opinion that a man's character was much sooner perceived in things of this sort than in what is done publicly and in open day. They chose, therefore, two persons, one out of the patricians, the other out of the commons, who were to watch, correct, and punish, if any one ran too much into voluptuousness, or transgressed the usual manner of life of his country; and these they called Censors. They had power to take away a horse, or expel out of the senate any one who lived intemperately and out of order. It was also their business to take an estimate of what every one was worth, and to put down in registers everybody's birth and quality; besides many other prerogatives. And therefore the chief nobility opposed his pretensions to it. Jealousy prompted the patricians, who thought that it would be a stain to everybody's nobility, if men of no original honour should rise to the highest dignity and power; while others, conscious of their own evil practices, and of the violation of the laws and customs of their country, were afraid of the austerity of the man; which, in an office of such great power, was likely to prove most uncompromising and severe. And so, consulting among themselves, they brought forward seven candidates in opposition to him, who sedulously set themselves to court the people's favour by fair promises, as though what they wished for was indulgent and easy government. Cato, on the contrary, promising no such mildness, but plainly threatening evil livers, from the very hustings openly declared himself, and exclaiming that the city needed a great and thorough purgation, called upon the people, if they were wise, not to choose the gentlest, but the roughest of physicians; such a one, he said, he was, and Valerius Flaccus, one of the patricians, another; together with him, he doubted not but he should do something worth the while, and that by cutting to pieces and burning like a hydra all luxury and voluptuousness. He added, too, that he saw all the rest endeavouring after the office with ill intent, because they were afraid of those who would exercise it justly, as they ought. And so truly great and so worthy of great men to be its leaders was, it would seem, the Roman people, that they did not fear the severity and grim countenance of Cato, but rejecting those smooth promisers who were ready to do all things to ingratiate themselves, they took him, together with Flaccus; obeying his recommendations not as though he were a candidate, but as if he had had the actual power of commanding and governing already.

Cato named, as chief of the senate, his friend and colleague Lucius Valerius Flaccus, and expelled, among many others, Lucius Quintius, who had been consul seven years before, and (which was greater honour to him than the consulship) brother to that Titus Flaminius who overthrew King Philip. . . .

His treatment of Lucius, likewise the brother of Scipio, and one who had been honoured with a triumph, occasioned some odium against Cato; for he took his horse from him, and was thought to do it with a design of putting an affront on Scipio Africanus, now dead. But he gave most general annoyance by retrenching people's luxury; for though (most of the youth being thereby already corrupted) it seemed almost impossible to take it away with an open hand and directly, yet going, as it were, obliquely around, he caused all dress, carriages, women's ornaments, household furniture, whose price exceeded one thousand five hundred drachmas, to be rated at ten times as much as they were worth; intending by thus making the assessments greater, to increase the taxes paid upon them. He also ordained that upon every thousand *asses* of property of this kind, three should be paid, so that people, burdened with these extra charges and seeing others of as good estates, but more frugal and sparing, paying less into the public exchequer, might be tried out of their prodigality. And thus, on the one side, not only those were disgusted at Cato who bore the taxes for the sake of their luxury, but those, too, who on the other side laid by their luxury for fear of the taxes. For people in general reckon that an order not to display their riches is equivalent to the taking away of their riches, because riches are seen much more in superfluous than in necessary things. Indeed this was what excited the wonder of Ariston the philosopher; that we account those who possess superfluous things more happy than those who abound with what is necessary and useful. But when one of his friends asked Scopas, the rich Thessalian, to give him some article of no great utility, saying that it was not a thing that he had any great need or use for himself, "In truth," replied he, "it is just these useless and unnecessary things that make my wealth and happiness." Thus the desire of riches does not proceed from a natural passion within us, but arises rather from vulgar out-of-doors opinion of other people.

Cato, notwithstanding, being little solicitous as to those

who exclaimed against him, increased his austerity. He caused the pipes, through which some persons brought the public water into their houses and gardens, to be cut, and threw down all buildings which jutted out into the common streets. He beat down also the price in contracts for public works to the lowest, and raised it in contracts for farming the taxes to the highest sum; by which proceedings he drew a great deal of hatred upon himself. Those who were of Titus Flaminius's party cancelled in the senate all the bargains and contracts made by him for the repairing and carrying on of the sacred and public buildings as unadvantageous to the commonwealth. They incited also the boldest of the tribunes of the people to accuse him and to fine him two talents. They likewise much opposed him in building the court or basilica, which he caused to be erected at the common charge, just by the senate-house, in the market-place, and called by his own name, the Porcian. However, the people, it seems, liked his censorship wondrously well; for, setting up a statue for him in the temple of the goddess of Health, they put an inscription under it, not recording his commands in war or his triumph, but to the effect that this was Cato the Censor, who, by his good discipline and wise and temperate ordinances, reclaimed the Roman commonwealth when it was declining and sinking down into vice. Before this honour was done to himself, he used to laugh at those who loved such kind of things, saying, that they did not see that they were taking pride in the workmanship of brass-founders and painters; whereas the citizens bore about his best likeness in their breasts. And when any seemed to wonder that he should have never a statue, while many ordinary persons had one, "I would," said he, "much rather be asked, why I have not one, than why I have one." In short, he would not have any honest citizen endure to be praised, except it might prove advantageous to the commonwealth. Yet still he had passed the highest commendation on himself; for he tells us that those who did anything wrong, and were found fault with, used to say it was not worth while to blame them, for they were not Catos. He also adds, that they who awkwardly mimicked some of his actions were called left-handed Catos; and that the senate in perilous times would cast their eyes on him, as upon a pilot in a ship, and that often when he was not present they put off affairs of greatest consequence. These things are indeed also testified of him by others; for he had a great authority in the city, alike for his life, his eloquence, and his age.

He was also a good father, an excellent husband to his wife, and an extraordinary economist; and as he did not manage his affairs of this kind carelessly, and as things of little moment, I think I ought to record a little further whatever was commendable in him in these points. He married a wife more noble than rich; being of opinion that the rich and the high-born are equally haughty and proud; but that those of noble blood would be more ashamed of base things, and consequently more obedient to their husbands in all that was fit and right. A man who beat his wife or child laid violent hands, he said, on what was most sacred; and a good husband he reckoned worthy of more praise than a great senator; and he admired the ancient Socrates for nothing so much as for having lived a temperate and contented life with a wife who was a scold, and children who were half-witted.

As soon as he had a son born, though he had never such urgent business upon his hands, unless it were some public matter, he would be by when his wife washed it and dressed it in its swaddling clothes. For she herself suckled it, nay, she often too gave her breast to her servants' children, to produce, by suckling the same milk, a kind of natural love in them to her son. When he began to come to years of discretion, Cato himself would teach him to read, although he had a servant, a very good grammarian, called Chilo, who taught many others; but he thought not fit, as he himself said, to have his son reprimanded by a slave, or pulled, it may be, by the ears when found tardy in his lesson: nor would he have him owe to a servant the obligation of so great a thing as his learning; he himself, therefore (as we were saying), taught him his grammar, law, and his gymnastic exercises. Nor did he only show him, too, how to throw a dart, to fight in armour, and to ride, but to box also and to endure both heat and cold, and to swim over the most rapid and rough rivers. He says, likewise, that he wrote histories, in large characters, with his own hand, that so his son, without stirring out of the house, might learn to know about his countrymen and forefathers. . . .

Thus, like an excellent work, Cato formed and fashioned his son to virtue; nor had he any occasion to find fault with his readiness and docility; but as he proved to be of too weak a constitution for hardships, he did not insist on requiring of him any very austere way of living. However, though delicate in health, he proved a stout man in the field, and behaved himself valiantly when Paulus Aemilius fought against Perseus; where when his sword was struck from him by a blow, or rather slipped out of his hand by reason of its moistness, he so keenly resented it, that he turned to some of his friends about him, and taking them along with him again fell upon the enemy; and having by a long fight and much force cleared the place, at length found it among great heaps of arms, and the dead bodies of friends as well as enemies piled one upon another. Upon which Paulus, his general, much commended the youth; and there is a letter of Cato's to his son, which highly praised his honourable eagerness for the recovery of his sword. Afterwards he married Tertia, Aemilius Paulus's daughter, and sister to Scipio; nor was he admitted into this family less for his own worth than his father's. So that Cato's care in his son's education came to a very fitting result.

. . . At first, when he was but a poor soldier, he would not be difficult in anything which related to his eating, but looked upon it as a pitiful thing to quarrel with a servant for the belly's sake; but afterwards, when he grew richer, and made any feasts for his friends and colleagues in office, as soon as supper was over he used to go with a leather thong and scourge those who had waited or dressed the meat carelessly. He always contrived, too, that his servants should have some difference one among another, always suspecting and fearing a good understanding between them. Those who had committed anything worthy of death, he punished if they were found guilty by the verdict of their fellow-servants. But being after all much given to the desire of gain, he looked upon agriculture rather as a pleasure than profit; resolving, therefore, to lay out his money in safe and solid things, he purchased ponds, hot baths, grounds full of fuller's earth, remunerative lands, pastures, and woods; from all which he drew large returns, nor could Jupiter himself, he used to say, do him much damage. He was also given to the form of usury, which is considered most odious, in traffic by sea; and that thus:—he desired that those whom he put out his money to should have many partners; when the number of them and their ships came to be fifty, he himself took one share through Quintio his freedman, who therefore was to sail with the adventurers, and take a part in all their proceedings, so that thus there was no danger of losing his whole stock, but only a little part, and that with a prospect of great profit. He likewise lent money to those of his slaves who wished to borrow, with which they bought also other young ones, whom, when they had taught and bred up at his charges, they would sell again at the year's end; but some of them Cato would keep for himself, giving just as much for them as another had offered. To incline his son to be of his kind or temper, he used to tell him that it was not like a man, but rather like a widow woman, to lessen an estate. But the strongest indication of Cato's avaricious humour was when he took the boldness to affirm that he was a most wonderful, nay, a godlike man, who left more behind him than he had received.

He was now grown old, when Carneades the Academic, and Diogenes the Stoic, came as deputies from Athens to Rome, praying for release from a penalty of five hundred talents laid on the Athenians, in a suit, to which they did not appear, in which the Oropians were plaintiffs and Sicyonians judges. All the most studious youth immediately waited on these philosophers, and frequently, with admiration, heard them speak. But the gracefulness of Carneades's oratory, whose ability was really greatest, and his reputation equal to it, gathered large and favourable audiences, and ere long filled, like a wind, all the city with the sound of it. So that it soon began to be told that a Greek, famous even to admiration, winning and carrying all before him, had impressed so strange a love upon the young men, that quitting all their pleasures and pastimes, they ran mad, as it were, after philosophy; which indeed much pleased the Romans in general; nor could they but with much pleasure see the youth receive so welcomely the Greek literature, and frequent the company of learned men. But Cato, on the other side, seeing the passion for words flowing into the city, from the beginning took it ill, fearing lest the youth should be diverted that way, and so should prefer the glory of speaking well before that of arms and doing well. And when the fame of the philosophers increased in the city, and Caius Acilius, a person of distinction, at his own request, became their interpreter to the senate at their first audience, Cato resolved, under some specious pretence, to have all philosophers cleared out of the city; and, coming into the senate, blamed the magistrates for letting these deputies stay so long a time without being despatched, though they were persons that could easily persuade the people to what they pleased; that therefore in all haste something should be determined about their petition, that so they might go home again to their own schools, and declaim to the Greek children, and leave the Roman youth to be obedient, as hitherto, to their own laws and governors.

Yet he did this not out of any anger, as some think, to Carneades; but because he wholly despised philosophy, and out of a kind of pride scoffed at the Greek studies and literature; as, for example, he would say, that Socrates was a prating, seditious fellow, who did his best to tyrannise over his country, to undermine the ancient customs, and to entice and withdraw the citizens to opinions contrary to the laws. Ridiculing the school of Isocrates, he would add, that his scholars grew old men before they had done learning with him, as if they were to use their art and plead causes in the court of Minos in the next world. And to frighten his son from anything that was Greek, in a more vehement tone than became one of his age, he pronounced, as it were, with the voice of an oracle, that the Romans would certainly be destroyed when they began once to be infected with Greek literature; though time indeed has shown the vanity of this his prophecy; as, in truth, the city of Rome has risen to its highest fortune while entertaining Grecian learning. Nor had he an aversion only against the Greek philosophers, but the physicians also; for having, it seems, heard how Hippocrates, when the king of Persia sent for him, with offers of a fee of several talents, said, that he would never assist barbarians who were enemies to the Greeks; he affirmed, that this was now become a common oath taken by all physicians, and enjoined his son to have a care and avoid them; for that he himself had written a little book of prescriptions for curing those who were sick in his family; he never enjoined fasting to any one, but ordered them either vegetables, or the meat of a duck, pigeon, or leveret; such kind of diet being of light digestion and fit for sick folks, only it made those who ate it dream a little too much; and by the use of this kind of physic, he said, he not only made himself and those about him well, but kept them so.

However, for this his presumption he seemed not to have escaped unpunished; for he lost both his wife and his son; though he himself, being of a strong, robust constitution, held out longer. . . . His eldest died in his praetorship; of whom Cato often makes mention in his books, as having been a good man. He is said, however, to have borne the loss moderately and like a philosopher, and was nothing the more remiss in attending to affairs of state; so that he did not, as Lucius Lucullus and Metellus Pius did, grow languid in his old age, as though public business were a duty once to be discharged, and then quitted; nor did he, like Scipio Africanus, because envy had struck at his glory, turn from the public, and change and pass away the rest of his life without doing anything; but as one persuaded Dionysius, that the most honourable tomb he could have would be to die in the exercise of his dominion; so Cato thought that old age to be the most honourable which was busied in public affairs; though he would, now and then, when he had leisure, recreate himself with husbandry and writing.

And, indeed, he composed various books and histories; and in his youth he addicted himself to agriculture for profit's sake; for he used to say he had but two ways of getting—agriculture and parsimony; and now, in his old age, the first of these gave him both occupation and a subject of study. He wrote one book on country matters, in which he treated particularly even of making cakes and preserving fruit; it being his ambition to be curious and singular in all things. His suppers, at his country house, used also to be plentiful; he daily invited his friends and neighbours about him, and passed the time merrily with them; so that his company was not only agreeable to those of the same age, but even to younger men; for he had had experience in many things, and had been concerned in much, both by word and deed, that was worth the hearing. He looked upon a good table as the best place for making friends; where the commendations of brave and good citizens were usually introduced, and little said of base and unworthy ones; as Cato would not give leave in his company to have anything, either good or ill, said about them.

Some will have the overthrow of Carthage to have been one of his last acts of state; when, indeed, Scipio the younger did by his valour give it the last blow, but the war, chiefly by the counsel and advice of Cato, was undertaken on the following occasion. Cato was sent to the Carthaginians and Masinissa, King of Numidia, who were at war with one another, to know the cause of their difference. He, it seems, had been a friend of the Romans from the beginning; and they, too, since they were conquered by Scipio, were of the Roman confederacy, having been shorn of their power by loss of territory and a heavy tax. Finding Carthage, not (as the Romans thought) low and in an ill condition, but well manned, full of riches and all sorts of arms and ammunition, and perceiving the Carthaginians carry it high, he conceived that it was not a time for the Romans to adjust affairs between them and Masinissa; but rather that they themselves would fall into danger, unless they should find means to check this rapid new growth of Rome's ancient irreconcilable enemy. Therefore, returning quickly to Rome, he acquainted the senate that the former defeats and blows given to the Carthaginians had not so much diminished their strength, as it had abated their imprudence and folly; that they were not become weaker, but more experienced in war, and did only skirmish with the Numidians to exercise themselves the better to cope with the Romans: that the peace and league they had made was but a kind of suspension of war which awaited a fairer opportunity to break out again.

Moreover, they say that, shaking his gown, he took occasion to let drop some African figs before the senate. And on their admiring the size and beauty of them, he presently added, that the place that bore them was but three days' sail from Rome. Nay, he never after this gave his opinion, but at the end he would be sure to come out with this sentence, "ALSO, CARTHAGE, METHINKS, OUGHT UTTERLY TO BE DESTROYED." But Publius Scipio Nasica would always declare his opinion to the contrary, in these words, "It seems requisite to me that Carthage should still stand." For seeing his countrymen to be grown wanton and insolent, and the people made, by their prosperity, obstinate and disobedient to the senate, and drawing the whole city, whither they would, after them, he would have had the fear of Carthage to serve as a bit to hold the contumacy of the multitude; and he looked upon the Carthaginians as too weak to overcome the Romans, and too great to be despised by them. On the other side, it seemed a perilous thing to Cato that a city which had been always great, and was now grown sober and wise, by reason of its former calamities, should still lie, as it were, in wait for the follies and dangerous excesses of the over-powerful Roman people; so that he thought it the wisest course to have all outward dangers removed, when they had so many inward ones among themselves.

Thus Cato, they say, stirred up the third and last war against the Carthaginians: but no sooner was the said war begun, than he died, prophesying of the person that should put an end to it who was then only a young man; but, being tribune in the army, he in several fights gave proof of his courage and conduct. The news of which being brought to Cato's ears at Rome, he thus expressed himself:—

> "The only wise man of them all is he,
> The others e'en as shadows flit and flee."

This prophecy Scipio soon confirmed by his actions.

Cato left no posterity, except one son by his second wife, who was named . . . Cato Salonius; and a grandson by his eldest son, who died. Cato Salonius died when he was praetor, but his son Marcus was afterwards consul, and he was grandfather of Cato the philosopher, who for virtue and renown was one of the most eminent personages of his time.

— *NOTES* —

NOTES